In Praise of WIREFRAMED

In WIREFRAMED, Vivek Sharma has created the essential companion for any business executive seeking to navigate the complex jumble of concepts and terminology of today's Digital Age. It is a well-organized and user-friendly blueprint that effectively draws on examples from Man's earliest times right up to the 2020 COVID pandemic to underscore its key points.

Ron Sugar, former CEO of Northrop Grumman, current board member at Chevron, Amgen and Apple and chairman of the board at Uber

For every business leader who has sat through meetings listening to digital strategists and understanding only a fraction of what has been said, WIREFRAMED is your equalizer. Read it, absorb it, pass it on. Delayed or deferred digital fluency is not an option. Read WIRE-FRAMED like your business depends on it – because it does.

Robin Hayes, CEO, JetBlue Airways

An exceptionally approachable and brisk blueprint for understanding the digital revolution and how to navigate it.

Steve Ellis, co-managing partner of TPG's The Rise Fund, current board member at Charles Schwab

With WIREFRAMED, Vivek Sharma provides an essential and ap-proachable primer for any business leader wanting a better grasp of what, why, where and how "digital" technologies are shaping our world.

Tom Staggs, former COO of The Walt Disney Co., current board member at Spotify

Vivek Sharma explains and simplifies what "digital" truly means in WIREFRAMED. Once readers become versed in the digital language, he focuses the book on the impact these concepts can have on our professional and personal lives. An entertaining, enlightening and thought-provoking read for anyone interested in digital's place in today's business world.

Amy Miles, former CEO of Regal Entertainment, current board member at Amgen and Gap

WIREFRAMED takes the complex subject of what it takes to lead the digital transformation of a business and distills it down to something every business leader can understand. From the straightforward definitions of what digital actually means, to the real world examples of companies that have successfully undertaken this journey, the book provides a practical way for business leaders to think through and execute digital innovation in the real world.

Mark Fields, former CEO, Ford Motor Co.; current board member, Qualcomm

WIREFRAMED

Simplifying Digital Innovation for Business Leaders

Vivek Sharma

Foreword by Secretary Ray Mabus

First editions, paperback and hard cover, September 2020

Cover design by PixelStudio

ISBN 978-1-7356223-1-6 (Paperback)
ISBN 978-1-7356223-2-3 (Hardback)
ISBN 978-1-7356223-0-9 (Ebook)

Independently published by Sairya LLC

Dedication

To my mother and father

आचार्यात् पादमादत्ते पादं शष्यि: स्वमेधया ।
सब्रह्मचारभ्यि: पादं पादं कालक्रमेण च ॥

One fourth from the teacher,
one fourth from own intelligence,
One fourth from fellow students,
and one fourth with the passage of time.

A Sanskrit verse on learning from the epic Mahabharata Udyoga Parva

Contents

Acknowledgments

This book arrives and stands on the shoulders of many dedicated, amazing people. For them, I am grateful in so many ways.

To Greys Sošić, Ramandeep Randhawa and Yehuda Bassok at the University of Southern California's Marshall School of Business Department of Data Science & Operations, thank you for your continued support as a leadership team.

To Brian MacDougall, thank you for your skill and diligence as the course manager for the USC Marshall course that serves as this book's inspiration: Digital Foundations in Business Innovation (DFBI). Thanks, too, for your editorial and research support on this manuscript. Thanks to Scott Blue for your role as editor and publishing adviser. Thank you also to John James Nicoletti for book publishing support.

To Daniel Altobello, Joe Chen, Doug Gilstrap, George Huang, Narayan Iyengar, James Kugler, Catherine Lepard, Aaron Martin, Colleen Monaco, Akshaya Moondra, Stefan Olander, Atif Rafiq, Judy Sewards and Jarett Smith, thank you for your contributions, support and talent serving as contributors to and interviewees for the USC Marshall School of Business blog, Wireframed. Your work helped make the blog a success and this book possible.

To Scott Andress, Naveen Baweja, Jorge Camargo, Jason Cox, Priyanka Kakar, Ed Kim, Tarun Malhotra, Emmanuel Marques, Rod Russell and Richard Webby, who helped as DFBI guest lecturers.

Your efforts created a master class in digital that serves as the foundation of this book.

Special thanks are reserved for Daniel Altobello, Jarett Smith and Colleen Monaco, who contributed to both Wireframed and the class lectures, and I so appreciate both efforts.

To the following, superlative individuals, I also send my heartfelt thanks: Kurt Besecker, Pat Binkley, Hugh Birch, Heather Bishop, Olivier Cadoret, Kelly Cheng, Jason Cox, Michael DeCook, Mark Dekunder, Scott DePriest, Sha Edathumparampil, Max Greenhut, Jeff Hall, Joey Hasty, Yas Inukai, Priyanka Kakar, Tim Klauda, Sarah Laiwala, Mark Liu, Mary Lowery, Vinay Moharil, Arvind Puri, Diane Ryan-Schaffer, Andrew Santelli, Jay Schneider, Steve Sullivan, Michael Trum, Mark Winkelbauer, Gemini Wong and Tamra Yoder.

Foreword

In any decision-making situation, in any leadership role, one of the absolutely crucial requirements is to be able to understand the context and the language involved. A prime differentiator among fields, specialties and professions are the words – the language – used. Nowhere is this more true than in the realm of "digital" in the business world. For business people who are not steeped in technology, and that accounts for a vast majority of those in business, even the term "digital" can be amorphous, confusing and daunting.

Learning how to grasp the concepts and use the language of something as big, swiftly changing and complex as digital can be seen by the ordinary person in business as difficult, if not impossible. Technical terms and jargon can be used as a way to exclude those with no understanding and cause decisions to be made on very imperfect information, which can lead to unwise, or even harmful, outcomes. If you do not know the language, the terms, the references, not only will your decisions be based on a foundational lack of knowledge, you cannot even follow or join the conversation in a meaningful way.

Vivek Sharma in this wonderful book, *WIREFRAMED*, has demystified it, organized it and made it not only understandable but also entertaining. For the uninitiated, the word "wireframed" is as mysterious as the world of new tech in general. Having a guidebook like *WIREFRAMED* means that you can confidently navigate this world.

I have very personal knowledge of what it is like to be thrust into a major decision-making role in a very large and complex environment with its own language without prior technical expertise. When I became Secretary of the Navy for the United States, I took over an organization with a more than 230-year history, 900,000 people and a budget of $170 billion. If the Department of the Navy, which includes the Navy and the Marines, were a private company, it would be one of the Fortune Five. My responsibilities were to do the business of "recruit, train and equip." Included in this was preparing, presenting and defending a massive budget each year and purchasing some of the most complicated and technologically sophisticated equipment on the planet.

As a college English major, I had stepped into one of the most technical jobs anywhere. The Pentagon loves acronyms and complexity and, early on, it was clear that those who were briefing and advising me were speaking in a tongue with which I was not familiar. The shorthand came fast and constant: FYDP (Future Years Defense Program – the next five years budget estimates which had to be done every year), FYSA (for your situational awareness) and BLUF (bottom line up front) were but a few of the more straightforward terms I had to understand quickly. There were many others which were far more specifically technical and not intuitive.

My education was strictly OJT (on the job training). I asked thousands of questions, stopped presentations when there was a term I didn't know (which was often) and did an enormous amount of homework. Of course, I was fortunate because I was in charge and could ask people to stop and explain. This isn't always possible in different contexts.

Vivek Sharma has spared everyone who reads this book the pain of what I had to do and of trying to penetrate on your own a tangled maze of terms and language. *WIREFRAMED* is well organized, gives relatable examples and explanations and should be read by anyone trying to decode "digital" in today's business world – which should be just about everyone.

WIREFRAMED is immensely valuable and incredibly well timed. Vivek Sharma has performed an essential service with this book.

The Honorable Ray Mabus
75th U.S. Secretary of the Navy (2009-2017)
U.S. Ambassador to Saudi Arabia (1994-1996)
60th Governor of Mississippi (1988-1992)

Introduction

Let's begin with you – your interactions and conversations about digital.

You find yourself on a plane where a colleague pings you with an article from *Forbes*. It's on the quickly evolving nature of artificial intelligence (AI). You skim it. There is a helpful analogy to understand how it works and then a substantive exploration of how this technology is transforming business. You file it or bookmark it. It's so outside of your frame of reference. You know it's essential, but you save it for later.

Later, over a weekend, you scroll the latest issue of *The Wall Street Journal* technology section over coffee. You read about deconstructing neural networks and how they have shaped or not shaped enterprise computing and where that's taking customer relationships and experience. It's fascinating. You grasp the words, but you struggle to recognize what this might mean for you, your company. That fact frustrates you.

Back at work, a group touting the impact and urgency of digital transformation attempts to engage senior leadership, and you're one of those leaders – or a high-potential rising star in the room. You use technology and grasp some of its evolution, but you don't speak the language.

In fact, at times, you feel lost. The group throws around phrases such as "blockchain," "APIs," "machine learning," "platform as a service" and "neural networks." Worse, they seamlessly understand and make assumptions around how digital technologies fuel exponential impact and foretell a depth and level of change that is exciting yet also so dramatic and exponential. It makes you and some of your counterparts feel uncomfortable and unsure.

Through it all, here's what you *do know*: Digital isn't new; it's not in the future. It's now, and it's not going away. You also know that to understand digital, you must first acquire the proper lens through which to view it. You need grounding in the basics. You're looking for a source that offers a newfound fluency and pulls that knowledge through key trends and industry applications so you can begin asking the important strategic questions. From there, you can contribute meaningfully to the dialogue around digital and how it should factor into corporate trajectory.

You, and many like you, have inspired *WIREFRAMED*. Wireframed is a digital term referring to a strategic blueprint that serves as a foundation used for dialogue. Wireframes offer a simple, easily understood overview that sparks dialogue and advances a final design. They also foreshadow this work's purpose. It's written for those with little or no technology or engineering background and yet who recognize that today, digital has become foundational to every industry, sector and job. It assumes that you and your organization need a basic working knowledge of digital before digital is deployable as a strategic asset. Further, it's written from firsthand experience and a core presupposition: Achieving the speed, sustainability and execution success through a digital transformation, for any organization, requires that all employees gain facility with the basics.

WIREFRAMED is inspired by a graduate course, "Digital Foundations for Business Innovation," which I teach at the University of Southern California's Marshall School of Business. Offered within the MBA and MSBA curricula, the course links to my Marshall blog focused on digital trends. It, too, is titled Wireframed. At USC, I can connect with an amazing and uncommonly gifted set of graduate-level students pulled from business, data science, communication, public policy, social work and computer sciences – individuals who represent the next generation of leadership across some critical disciplines.

In course form, I fast-track fluency in the "language framework of digital" as a tool for business innovation. Many students have some familiarity with digital but aren't comfortable "talking the talk." Therefore, I designed the course to help students engage in dialogue with one another and with executive guest speakers, primarily centering on how emerging digital tools and technologies of our time can provide opportunities and challenges for business leaders.

What I've learned from these students as they form their digital foundation is that at some point in the journey, they are imbued with the confidence to engage on these topics on their own terms. They also begin wielding these digital technologies to advance their original thought and transform their businesses. In this way, students have reflected back to me the fact that beyond talking the talk, they can begin walking the walk. This book is, in large part, designed to do the same within a self-learning setting, and I believe it arrives at a clear inflection point.

WIREFRAMED is going to press against the backdrop of the global COVID-19 pandemic. Due to the shutdown of nonessential businesses and the activation of work-from-home and distance learning plans across organizations and institutions, digital has formed the connective tissue for commerce, education and social life across continents. The medical community and pharmaceutical industry are leveraging digital to track, study and find a vaccine for the virus. At no point in history have we relied on digital to do so much. In turn, it's accelerating its integration into work and life.

I've organized *WIREFRAMED* into three parts that unify and build on experiences at my previous firms, USC and within the Wireframed blog:

Part 1: "The Intelligent Machine" takes you deep inside the workings and evolution of digital. It blueprints digital by humanizing it. It then introduces how the Intelligent Machine works from a dynamic digital foundation composed of five building blocks: storing, computing, software, connecting and sensing. We break down each building block and discuss how they complement each other while exponentially driving major digital trends.

Part 2: "The Machine in Action" backs out of the machine proper to see how it works and how it's spawning seven key digital trends: big data, the cloud, cybersecurity, artificial intelligence, augmented and virtual reality, digital currency and, finally, the post-screen IoT world. Through each, we will seek to understand in the simplest terms the arc and implications of the trends while using recent industry examples.

Part 3: "Phygital" goes strategically high level, introduces the speed with which the physical and digital worlds are overlapping and shows how that fact is fundamentally transforming key industries. It explains why this convergence is accelerating, by dissecting five sectors: health care and pharmaceutical, financial services, automobiles, government and retail. We then examine how phygital is driving whole-industry disruption and overlooked terrain: white-collar environments. As in Part 2, our focus will be on simplicity, timeliness and comprehensibility.

Note, readers steeped in technical knowledge may find sections of this book too simplistic. They might also complain it lacks specific technical details they expect. They might view topics and examples selected as very subjective. I would acknowledge upfront that these observations are indeed valid. If you're picking this up as a digitally acute purist, *WIREFRAMED* may come across as too remedial and technically inelegant. That's on purpose, as you are not the intended reader of this book.

My goal here is comprehension in the simplest terms for someone with little or no digital background. This book is about inspiring them to embark on a self-guided journey of learning. It is a "101" for motivated learners.

If, after experiencing this book, said learners feel confident in their understanding of the digital ecosystem and build on that initial understanding through an even deeper self-educational process, then I have succeeded with this effort.

Vivek Sharma
September 2020

Part 1
The Intelligent Machine

Intelligence requires dexterity – dexterity at the intersection of acquiring knowledge and putting that knowledge into action. It reflects the ability to absorb, reflect on and execute a series of skills. It's the stuff of living, breathing creatures, and it's the obsession of humanity. We are born to learn.

Since our dawn as a species, we've been developing, evolving and putting intelligence to use in direct service to surviving and thriving on this planet. Imagine an animated timeline that begins with the earliest humans discovering fire. Zoom in to a celebration of the first wheel. Move through the metallic ages. Join traders on the Silk Road. Watch a firework illuminate the Great Wall. Fly past the Acropolis, dip into the Renaissance and then head north to see Queen Elizabeth I taking in Shakespeare's *A Midsummer Night's Dream*. Flow through to the Industrial Revolution. Then move skyward beyond our atmosphere and witness a module docking with the International Space Station. Now descend quickly back to earth and focus on a child Googling these moments in history on the most leading-edge consumer technology you can imagine. The human capacity for drawing on history to envision the future while informing the present has resulted in centuries of applied intelligence.

Therefore, any talk of digital must begin with recognizing it as a unique creation of humanity. The easiest way to understand it is to map its building blocks against the center of our intelligence: the human brain. Its physiology is the model for a majority of technological breakthroughs.

Here's a case in point: In the 19th century, Spanish Nobel laureate Santiago Ramón y Cajal was a pioneer in neuroanatomy. He thoroughly and systematically began detailing the cerebral cortex and neurons. One century later, his thinking guided Americans Warren McCulloch, a psychologist, and Walter Pitts, a mathematical savant. These two collaborated in the 1940s to figure out how neurons functioned. They hypothesized that it came down to a simple binary decision of answering a query with "true" or "false." While research has since shown that neurological reality is much more nuanced, these early explorations of neural function ultimately road-mapped the architecture of the first modern computer. Perhaps you've heard of 1s and 0s that drive computing? It's a descendant of this thinking.

Taking this a step further, let's compare the brain and an intelligent machine. The brain consists of five lobes – the frontal, parietal and occipital lobes array to form the top layer from front to back. Tucked underneath is the temporal lobe, and further beneath both it and the occipital lobe, nestled next to the brain stem, is the cerebellum. These lobes and the stem connect to the spinal cord. Together they drive thinking, the five senses and all the systems of the body.

Five building blocks comprise the intelligent machine: storing, computing, software-initiated decisioning and action grounded in logic, connecting and sensing, all of which harmonize and mobilize a given system. Through intricate combinations activated by electricity, these building blocks act and interact in ways that are so similar to our neurology, and we can overlay them onto specific parts of the human brain.

Storage in the human brain correlates to human memory and knowledge resident in the frontal and temporal lobes. Computing, equated to thinking, mostly sits in the frontal lobe. The language and logic from and through which we act and speak – our software – reside in the temporal lobe. Connectivity that drives feelings, empathy, community and relationship, while facilitating two-way communication, is housed in the connections, called synapses, across more than 90 billion neurons and the spinal cord. Sensing takes place through sight, smell, taste, touch and sound, which courses through the spinal cord and into the brain stem. It is given primal voice through the cerebellum and undergoes refinement through the other lobes. Intelligent, no?

Now, imagine a laptop laid out before you, its lid opened to reveal the keyboard and screen. Inside this intelligent machine sits its elegant guts, securely soldered together. Let's map out the building blocks. On this device, storage correlates to random access memory (RAM) and hard drive memory. Computing happens through a central processing unit (CPU) and graphics processors. Software, represented by the operating system (OS) and specific apps, from music to email to word processing, orchestrates activity while using the machine. Connectivity that equips the machine for two-way communication comes in many forms on the laptop, ranging from wireless capabilities such as WiFi and Bluetooth to wire-ready ethernet, USB, micro USB or Thunderbolt. The laptop also contains sensors – a camera, keyboard, trackpad and built-in microphones.

Let's shrink this analogy. Pick up your iPhone or Android smartphone. It holds the same cartography as the laptop, only it's smaller and possibly the most-used device on the planet and indeed a tool around which many lives revolve. It has a lot of storage, for such a small device. Tiny but mighty, it executes so many functions we need, day after day. Software "apps" are a big part of that, and this is a device bursting with connectivity. Smartphones apply the forces foundational to digital in similar ways to the laptop. However, two things set it apart. First, it is an intelligent machine that takes sensing to a new level, as it is packed with elements for communication, navigation, environmental understanding and even a flashlight. Second, note its size in direct proportion to its power. It's a powerful Intelligent Machine and a beacon for how digital is evolving in both potency and size, and later in this section, we'll reveal the reason for that.

With the terrain of digital technology fully charted and locked away in your frontal and temporal lobes, it's time to examine each dynamic building block in detail.

1.1 Storage:
The Story of Memory

When we consume or create digital information, it accumulates somewhere. We read a document on Google Drive. We write something in Word. We browse a website. We stream music or a video. We take a selfie. Resulting digital data from this activity gets housed in sequential binary bits – a state of 0 or 1. It's called storage.

In our day-to-day lives, we tend to be conscious of storage in three ways: 1) When we look for, find, download, work with, save or organize something on a digital device and are informed of the size of a given piece of data such as a document or a music file. 2) When we install a software app and receive notification about how much storage the app requires. 3) When we are suddenly warned of a problem (maybe our device slows down or an app freezes; perhaps we get a warning signal from the device that it's about to run out of storage capacity; maybe we get an email from our cloud service provider saying it's time to delete files or upgrade our storage capacity).

A building block marked by capacity, storage volume is measured in bytes. A single byte, the smallest quantifiable unit of storage, is typically composed of eight bits. It is expressed in multiples of bytes as follows:

1,000 bytes = a kilobyte (KB)

1 million bytes = a megabyte (MB)

1 billion bytes = a gigabyte (GB)

1 trillion bytes = a terabyte (TB)

1 sextillion bytes = a zettabyte (ZB)

Every digital device – including the laptop and smartphone we examined in the previous chapter– contains primary and secondary storage. RAM is primary, offering temporary warehousing – like a backpack – that delivers quick access to data when that device is powered on.

Secondary storage, also known as device "memory," permanently archives data. It's less like a backpack and more like a shed. Available without a power supply, it works across an array of file genres, including a device's operating system software, applications and multimedia. So it is with any digital device, whether it's in a smartphone, a personal computer, a datacenter or the cloud.

Storage is foundational to computing capacity and speed. Like nearly every building block, it started big on the outside and small on the inside. As these attributes flip, with internal capacity increasing and external size decreasing, an intelligent machine can do more and do it faster.

Miniaturization over the last five decades is staggering. Let's start at nearly the beginning by painting a picture using the award-winning TV drama series *Mad Men*.

In a season seven episode titled "The Monolith," it's 1969. The lead character, Don Draper, enters the Manhattan offices of ad agency SC&P only to be confronted by a machine that has taken up residence in what had been the firm's "creative lounge" for copywriters.

It's the revolutionary IBM System/360 computer: a room-filling beast that strikes a space-age retro pose. In this episode, the S/360's depiction is that of an automation powerhouse that will make advertisers more intelligent, pumping out data that can answer critical market research questions in an era of mass media. Yet for modern viewers, the S/360's functionality is eclipsed by its form. Its sheer heft is jaw-dropping.

What dominates the S/360's massive footprint? Storage. Fronted by rows of giant, refrigerator-size boxes, the S/360 was topped with what looked like reel-to-reel tapes. Some remained stationary. Some spun up and rotated. Evolved versions of the earliest storage medium, magnetic tape, they resembled audiocassette tapes that emerged around the same time. Information was stored as a series of binary 1s or 0s on a thin polymer substrate through the presence or absence of magnetic polarity.

Magnetic tape storage is still with us mainly because of its enhanced security – tapes are stored offline and are relatively immune to cyberattacks. They are ideal for backup and archival applications. In 2011, Google's Gmail experienced a software bug impacting all digital copies of Gmail user data. Fortunately, Google had backed up using tapes, and, even though it took more than 30 hours, the company was able to restore full account access to customers.

In the mid-1950s, IBM augmented its line of polymer substrate storage technology with hard disk drives (HDDs, also known as floppy disks). Similar to how it was stored on tapes, digital information was stored by magnetizing disks in positive or negative polarity in precise locations. Manufacturers invested millions of dollars in research and development centered on miniaturization. They used nanophysics to increase speed and ruggedization. As such, HDDs eclipsed tapes in popularity. Optical storage is a newer variety of HDD technology. Laser beams and optical reflection store and retrieve information. This shift in technology increased speed and required fewer parts. Music and data CDs, DVDs for multimedia content and Blu-ray Discs for high-definition videos are examples of optical storage.

HDDs in all flavors have one major disadvantage: Inherently mechanical, their moving parts cause wear and tear on device storage units while generating heat, vibration and noise. A new storage medium solves these issues.

Solid-state drives (SSDs), also known as flash drives, use a processor (called a controller) to read and write data. Because it is solid-state, it has no moving parts. Compared to HDDs, flash drives are faster, lighter, quieter and more durable. They are also 10-50 times more expensive. Even so, SSDs are the new storage standard across devices.

In addition to storage media, storage location has evolved. In *Mad Men's* IBM System/360, all of the data resided on the machine. Over time, external hard drives, disk drives and flash drives allowed the warehousing of data outside the machine, increasing volume without requiring data deletion or device replacement. Over the last decade, the cloud has risen: remote storage offered as a service. Major cloud players such as Dropbox, Google Drive, Microsoft OneDrive and Apple's iCloud provide consumers and businesses storage opportunities that correlate price to volume.

In each case above, storage medium innovation has compressed increasing amounts of data on ever-decreasing units of physical space – or, in the case of the cloud, it's altogether eliminated the need for physical space.

Let's compare the IBM System/360 tapes to Western Digital's (WD) SanDisk microSD™ card. SanDisk is a storage pioneer founded in 1988 and subsequently purchased by WD. Perhaps your smartphone included an installed microSD™ or an equivalent competitive card to accommodate your capturing of photos and videos.

In 2005, SanDisk debuted the microSD™ card. It fit on a fingertip and could store 128MB, enough space for still images and audio but not a movie. Just 15 years later, in 2020, you can purchase a microSD™ of that same size, called a SanDisk Extreme, and store 1TB of data. It can bank 500 hours of movies. Comparatively staggering.

It proves even more staggering when we return to our *Mad Men* example. The room-filling IBM System/360 computer I referenced included a maximum storage capacity of *8MB* – what today would be the equivalent of nearly three audio files. Often, even large installations would top off at *216KB*. One high-resolution photo is around 175KB. Interestingly, tapes leveraged by the 360 – its storage medium – have also advanced, increasing information density per unit area of polymer by 30% *every year* for the last few decades. IBM recently demonstrated a new miniaturized tape storage technology that could record 201GB per square inch. A palm-size IBM tape cartridge holds 330TB of data. You'd have enough movies for the rest of your life.

This miniaturization often simplifies design and manufacturing output, which leads to a steep drop in cost. In 1960, 1GB of storage cost $2 million. In 1980, it decreased to $200,000. By the early 2000s, it was $7.70. Today, 1GB of storage costs just $0.009 – less than 1 cent. Sometimes, on the cloud, for consumers, it's even free.

At a corporate level, enterprise storage has depended upon on-site datacenters. Not anymore. Many companies have moved to hybrid storage solutions that include all storage media outlined above, plus the cloud, to maximize capabilities, security and access.

These innovations and the new economics of storage are not just shifting how we store; they are changing how *much* we store. According to storage leader Seagate, in 2019 the world stored less than 1 percent of its data. By 2025, it will increase by more than 400% – from 45ZB to

200ZB. Many corporations and governments store all of their data and don't routinely purge files. They have the capacity, and they're keeping their data.

An increased appetite for storage creates an interesting dilemma as we move beyond 2025. For all of the ongoing improvements in storage density and cost, current technologies might not be enough to support the ever-increasing demand for capacity. By 2040, all microchip-grade silicon in the world will have been exhausted, fully consumed. It raises the question as to whether there is a non-silicon innovation that could prove viable and innovate storage moving forward.

Right now, human DNA provides the likeliest blueprint. It has reliably warehoused genetic code for millions of years. Currently, digital information expresses data in a series of 0s and 1s. DNA stores information in combinations of five chemical bases, and researchers are testing ways to translate data's binary digital code into combinations of these bases. It would take just 10 tons of DNA to store the world's data, which could fit onto a semitractor-trailer.

While DNA storage is currently slow and expensive, judging by the history of technology, this might not be a problem for long. It also underscores how critical storage is to an intelligent machine. It's a building block marked by volume that archives data. Its ability to shrink physically while expanding internal capacity has driven costs down. It also equips a digital device to do more with greater fluidity, and this could shift dramatically in so many ways should it be stored on a molecule.

With that in mind, it's time to explore the building block that is the engine of an intelligent machine: computing.

1.2 Computing:
The Story of Speed

Computing is a catalyst within an intelligent machine. Every action you experience or initiate on your computer, from starting it up to accessing browsers and software apps, running those apps and typing or texting, is powered by a central processing unit (CPU) and graphics processors. They form the foundation of computing.

Traditional computing works through a switch connected to an integrated circuit of multiple silicon transistors on a single chip. Transistors switch between two binary states, 0 and 1, and this is how computing operates, with the binary 0 and 1 representing the language of computers. A single chip could consist of millions of transistors simultaneously switching, making the computer go. Net computing power is equal to the number of transistors.

Since the mid-1960s, computing power has doubled every 18 months. It's called Moore's Law. Developed by Gordon Moore, who co-founded Intel, a technology company responsible for a majority of processors inside today's digital devices, his original projection covered a time frame between 1965 and 1975. It continues to this day, unabated.

The number of transistors on a chip drives Moore's law. In 1971, the Intel 4004 processor carried 2,300 transistors. In 1995, the Intel Pentium Pro processor increased that number to 5.5 million. In 2016, the last time Intel disclosed transistor totals in its specifications, the 22-core Xeon Broadwell-E5 processor included 7.2 billion transistors.

The ability to shrink the size of a processor while increasing the number of transistors housed within it fueled the personal computing revolution. Just like with storage, smaller computers with ever-faster chips led to efficient, less expensive manufacturing. In 2005, a typical laptop with baseline features – 1.2 GHz processor and 500MB of RAM – cost slightly more than $1,000. Its "guts" would fill the entire volume of the laptop body that included a keyboard and screen. Today, UK-based nonprofit Raspberry has created the Pi series of computers. The Raspberry Pi 3 provides the same level of computing power as the 2005 laptop, but it also includes more RAM. It's the size of a credit card and costs $35. Raspberry's slightly more advanced Pi 4 offers a 1.5 GHz processor and up to 8GB of RAM. It costs $75. Both machines feature wireless and Bluetooth connectivity. When you receive the Pi, you insert an SD card, the older cousin of the SanDisk MicroSD card we discussed in Storage. Then you plug in a keyboard and a monitor, and it's ready to boot up.

Chip size has also decreased. IBM recently launched the world's first 5NM chip. That's nanometers, and it equals .000005 millimeters. In addition to transistors, it includes storage, connectivity and a camera. It's the same size as a common housefly. Going a step further, Seagate is in development with a 3NM chip. Eventually, when installed into smartphones or other devices, these chips will drive current intelligent machines into obsolescence. These tiny chips are not without their issues, and the challenges they've materialized have inspired the next great leap in computing: quantum.

Quantum Computing

As smaller, higher caliber machines drive computing's future, quantum computing offers a radical solution to traditional computing's challenges brought about through ever-smaller chips. It's poised to redefine computing velocity, and it's critical to grasping the future of computing.

Quantum takes speed to a different level – an atomic level – and it solves two critical problems facing traditional computing: quantum tunneling and the end of commercial-grade silica to make CPUs – the chips that make traditional computers go.

The IBM 5NM chip poised to redefine the market must prove its viability. In traditional computing, current dimensions of the smallest commercially available transistor are 10NM, equivalent in size to a few atoms. It's at this point we veer into the mind-bending topic of quantum mechanics. At 10 nanometers or smaller, electrons harnessed within transistor circuits run the risk of physically burrowing through to the chip's exterior. It's called quantum tunneling. When it happens, computing breaks down.

Quantum computing addresses tunneling by eliminating transistors. Instead, quantum computers use the spin orientation of elementary particles as the basis of computing. Electrons, the negatively charged particle that orbits the nucleus of an atom, fit the bill. In quantum, an electron spinning in one direction receives a value of 1. A spin in the other direction gets assigned the 0 value. Amazingly in the quantum world, and unlike traditional computing, the elementary particle – in this case the single electron – can hold both. It's a state known as superposition. Superposition expands the amount of information encoded on a single electron. Known as a qubit (quantum bit), it can represent either 0 or 1 or any combination of 0 and 1. It also increases speed. In traditional computing, any given action requires four steps. Through superposition, quantum requires just one.

Taking superposition a step further, traditional computers built with "n" bits execute 2^n the number of computations for every single n-bit quantum computation. A 30-qubit quantum computer's power is equivalent to a 10-teraflop classical computer (a device that can handle 1 trillion calculations per second) – a quantum leap in terms of speed and complexity.

The implications are beyond enormous. Applying quantum computing to commercial and scientific applications, where searching large datasets is an everyday task, quantum machines take a blink of time compared with traditional devices. This warp speed will change industries, empowering simulations of complex molecules for drug development, real time rebalancing of investment portfolios and optimization of logistics networks even during peak demand. With that much opportunity, why are quantum computers not already available commercially? The technical details follow, but in simple terms, it comes down to the extreme cold under which these intelligent machines need to work.

Because quantum computing involves isolating elementary particles such as an electron, electrons that get tangled together can begin leaking data. Not good. To make sure this doesn't happen, they are isolated. Achieving isolation requires cooling electrons down to 20 millikelvins (about -459 degrees Fahrenheit). Furthermore, isolation necessitates an elaborate infrastructure that exclusively exists in universities or research arms of leading technology firms. In essence, quantum is having its IBM System/360 moment, and as more funding flows, quantum will inevitably trace the same path to miniaturization and commercialization as traditional computing.

In that journey exists a much-anticipated milestone: the building of a 50-qubit computer. This innovation will usher in "quantum supremacy," that moment when traditional computers will not be able to match the speed of their quantum counterparts. It will also become an inflection point for data privacy and security. Here's why: Most internet encryption and authentication happen through public-key cryptography, which is essentially a mathematics problem too complicated for a current, traditional computer to solve. Public keys work by deploying one key for encrypting a message and one key for decrypting it. In an email, it means a sender's device leverages the encryption key to secure the message, converting it into "ciphertext" for dispatch across a network. The receiver device leverages the decryption key and decodes the ciphertext into the original message. The most recent estimate for overcoming the public key formula with a traditional intelligent machine is 173 years. A hacker with a 50-qubit computer could solve it within three seconds.

Quantum ensures the constant evolution of digital computing. It will be lightning-fast, and it will leverage access to that speed in the ways that contextually make sense in terms of use and cost. It also raises a leading question. What are we doing with all of the data accessed by all of that power? The third building block, software, answers most of that question.

1.3 Software:
The Story of Digital Self-Expression

Why is software considered a building block for an intelligent machine? Recall your life 20 years ago. What did it take to be digitally relevant? To be living at the leading edge of integrating technology into your daily life? The list would have included the following slate of digital devices:

Desktop and/or laptop for the web, email and all computing functions.

Television, cable or satellite and a DVD or Blue-Ray Disc player for movies.

Stereo and a design-forward "tower" for storing music and audiobook CDs.

The Apple iPod or another MP3 player for loading music or ripping and burning your CDs to facilitate listening to music on the go.

Cellular phone – preferably a "flip" – that had texting capability.

Dashboard-mountable GPS device for navigating without using MapQuest printouts.

E-reader for consuming books, magazines and newspapers.

Nintendo 360 and Nintendo Game Boy for at-home and portable gaming.

Digital camera.

Digital organizer such as a PalmPilot for note taking and life organization.

Now, pick up your smartphone. All of the devices mentioned above and their functions – their hardware and software – were aggregated onto this single device. That's thanks to what's called a software mega-platform hosted on an uncommonly intelligent machine driven by familiar names such as Apple iOS, Google Android or Windows Phone. Think of it as "cannibalization by smartphonification."

What is a platform? For our purposes, let's define it as software that serves at least 500 million active users. Within software development circles, it is said that platforms always beat products – in this case, that product is a single-use or discrete software application. That's because platforms orchestrate user and developer ecosystems that, if all goes to plan, scale, offer revenue diversity and dominate a market.

Today, a lot of companies are vying for platform status because it has never taken less time to eclipse that magic 500 million threshold. That's a relatively new phenomenon.

In the 1990s, Microsoft Office reached platform status in two decades following its introduction in and evolution through the 1970s. Microsoft Internet Explorer, which has undergone a relaunch in an attempt to reconnect with users, became a platform after eight years on the market. In the 2000s, Windows XP took 12 years.

Then, suddenly, acceleration intensified. Between 2000 and 2008, Facebook (2002) and the Apple iPhone Operating System (2007) made it in six years. Shortly thereafter, Google Android (2006) and What's App (2008) both made it in five years. In 2009, Google's Chrome browser made it in a previously unheard of three years. WeChat (2012) made it in four years. Instagram, aided by Facebook's acquisition, made it in seven. Then, in 2018, TikTok, the Chinese-based video app that allows users to take 15-second clips of footage, passed more than 500 million users in two years – 24 months! In 2020, it grew to more than

800 million users and offered significant distraction for the COVID-19 shelter in place phase. This collapse in time-to-platform highlights how software is a building block upon which digital is directly impacting how we live, learn and work.

Today, and beyond both mega-platform aggregation and time-to-platform compression, software moved through a defining moment that forever changed its deployment and usage: an innovation known as an API.

APIs (Application Programming Interface)

An application programming interface eliminates the need for having software on your device. Instead, you get a device-based interface, and the software – sometimes lots of it – runs elsewhere. APIs are close to revolutionary, and they are generating user experiences that have taken differentiation and disruption down entirely new roads – literally.

If you are one of the 111 million monthly Uber riders, you've experienced this firsthand, by seamlessly locating, ordering, tracking and paying for a taxi service, all from a few taps on your smartphone. Behind this front-end convenience lies a lot of real time coordination between Uber and multiple technology providers.

When you request a ride on your Uber iPhone app, Uber invokes Apple's Core Location framework to understand your location and then Apple's MapKit framework to show your real time location on the map. Once the driver has accepted the ride request, Uber uses Apple's notifications to advise you on the details of the car and the driver. It also provides the estimated time of arrival. While creating your Uber profile earlier, you would have used PayPal's Card.Io API framework to scan your credit card, which the app uses to process your payment through the Braintree API.

While building the Uber app, the developers at Uber didn't forge partnerships with Apple, Braintree and PayPal on how information gets queried, retrieved and used. Instead, Uber effectively outsourced its requirements for real time data, functionality and services by accessing each provider's API. As the name "application program interface" suggests, an API refers to an interface that allows the data and functionality of one software to be used by another software through a set of agreed-to standards. The API is not a new concept – around since computing's dawn. In the last 15 years, it's come into its own.

According to API Hound, today there are more than 50,000 APIs on the web, the majority of which are network APIs. That means they allow a developer to access information from a remote third-party system via the internet. Network APIs are increasingly monetized by the providers who build them, either on a per transaction basis or on a fee-for-service basis. This API economy holds three drivers fueling rapid growth and making APIs an even more disruptive powerhouse in digital.

First, even the most profitable firms do not have unlimited resources to focus on every business opportunity in their industry universe. Opening up APIs can drive revenue growth because they enable organizations to reach new users, channels and markets. Bala Iyer and Mohan Subramaniam documented this growth in a *Harvard Business Review* blog, reporting that Salesforce.com generates 50% of its revenue through APIs, eBay generates 60% and Expedia.com makes 90%. Salesforce cultivated an AppExchange marketplace on its platform that carries more than 300 apps. Expedia's APIs facilitate travel expenditures on flights, cars and hotel rooms via third-party apps. Through its APIs, eBay can list its auctions on other websites while accessing bidder information about sold items, stewarding transaction feedback and listing new items for sale – effectively expanding its footprint and revenue, free of charge.

Second, APIs help accelerate innovation by empowering developers to piggyback on multiple quality services while eliminating the investment of time and money in from-scratch building. Efficiency increases, and developers can rapidly create higher-level functionality for their customers.

Google Maps APIs offer a case in point. According to rough estimates, it would cost $8 billion to build an equivalent map product and additional millions of ongoing annual expenses to update images or monitor for inappropriate content. For a fraction of that cost, developers can use Google Maps APIs on a pay-per-use basis and take advantage of innovative features such as autocomplete, a location finder, real time traffic information and distance measurement. In this way, APIs have improved developer innovation exponentially. According to TechCrunch, more than 9 million developers are working on public APIs and another 1.2 million on private APIs.

APIs also drive quality and, if well-timed, a lucrative exit. Developers within the API ecosystem keep an eye on each other, especially when a third-party developer creates something using an API that surpasses its originator's product. Twitter did so with TweetDeck. Millions adopted it, favoring its interface, user experience and aesthetic. Developers loved it. Eventually, Twitter bought TweetDeck. Recognizing TweetDeck's superiority, Twitter shortcut the improvement of its user experience.

This same inspiration carries over to new technologies such as AI and MLR. Both require lots of training from high-quality datasets before commercial readiness. To that end, opening up APIs to the ecosystem has been the preferred approach for Google Prediction, IBM Watson, Amazon Machine Learning and Microsoft Azure cognitive services. Developers use the APIs tied to these technologies, and, in turn, the API originators get the datasets they need.

We've talked a lot here about developers crafting amazing apps leveraging APIs. On that note, software owes so much of its growth and renaissance to the next building block in the intelligent machine: connectivity.

1.4 Connecting:
The Story of Digital Contact

Connectivity is a unique building block within an intelligent machine because its rise made inroads for many of the other innovations we've already mentioned, including cloud storage, cloud computing, the growth of the API and, in the next chapter, sensing.

Up to this point, the best example of connectivity's potency rests in "cannibalization from smartphonification." Before seamless connectivity, as in wireless access across Bluetooth, WiFi and cellular networks, more devices and different forms of wired connectivity such as USB, ethernet and even old school CD-ROMS were required to update or expand hardware capabilities. Aggregating them onto a single, relatively tiny rectangle composed of plastic and Gorilla Glass would have proved impossible. That's because to do so requires an entire product development approach that presupposes wireless.

The wireless ecosystem itself developed through a series of technologies that furnish device connectivity over varying distances and applications. Near field communication (NFC) and its faster, more powerful cousin Bluetooth provide short-range connectivity between devices. WiFi offers wireless internet and local area network connectivity through a larger footprint via communication between a device's wireless card and a corresponding wireless router plugged into a network. Cellular networks provide long-range mobile connectivity through a network of transceivers that take connections wired to it and amplify them to mobile devices.

Wireless is advancing at the speed of light. Literally. LiFi is a high speed optical wireless technology that leverages an LED light source. It will prove especially handy in scenarios that are WiFi-averse – such as a hospital where mobile devices and traditional WiFi can interfere with medical equipment. WiGig advances WiFi using a frequency that enables ultra-fast connectivity and will prove critical for the advancement of high-volume data transmission such as augmented or virtual reality. WiFi HaLow is a slow but long-range form of WiFi that will be crucial to Internet of Things (IoT) communication. In terms of cellular advancements, there is 5G. It is a game-changer that will transform connectivity and even the geopolitical power structure of the next century. It's worth a deep dive.

5G Connectivity

"We're at the dawn of something new that will define the next decade and generation of connectivity," said Andre Fuetsch, chief technology officer, AT&T Communications, at the company's launch of a $145 billion network investment to what would bring 5G to 12 cities. "Mobile 5G will jump-start the next wave of unforeseen innovation."

Mobile tech giant Qualcomm has reinforced this breakthrough, estimating that the 5G value chain, from original equipment manufacturers and operators to content creators, app developers and consumers, could generate $3.5 trillion in revenue and 22 million jobs by 2035.

To truly understand 5G, let's trace the history of the Gs – BeeGees not included. Cell phones in the 1980s were 1G devices, delivering analog voice communication at maximum speeds of 2.4 Kbps. In the early 1990s, 2G devices offered digital voice communication and SMS/MMS at maximum speeds of 50 Kbps. As these devices evolved in the late 1990s, 3G technology included video calling and mobile internet capabilities, with an increased maximum data transmission speed of 3 Mbps. Finally, today's 4G (also called long-term evolution [LTE]) supports applications that demand maximum data transmission speed of 1 Gbps, such as gaming and video conferencing.

Fifth-generation cellular technology – that's what 5G stands for – has improved upon these previous generations of connectivity in terms of speed, higher bandwidth and ultra-low latency. Its estimated peak speed ranges from 1 Gbps to a staggering 20 Gbps. At 20 Gbps, a movie can download in three seconds. It can also deliver speed under load, and that's important.

As demand for data transmission has increased, bandwidth has become a problem that only 5G can solve. Because it uses incredibly small wavelengths, it can expand bandwidth availability, and it can do something called network-slicing that matches varying needs using a common network infrastructure. For example, it can simultaneously deliver extremely low latency for self-driving cars while providing extremely high data speeds for video streaming.

We talked about latency in conjunction with the cloud and edge computing, and 5G will do its part to improve it, making instantaneous, real time connectivity a reality by reducing latency to between one and three milliseconds. As we discussed before, minimizing latency is critical to expanding and making viable IoT. It's not just a speed issue. The volume of devices accessing connectivity at once can also impact it. On that front, 5G arrives with an expectation that it will support up to 1 million connected devices per square kilometer.

With all the great things 5G offers, why is adoption not happening with equal swiftness? It begins with smartphone manufacturers. With 5G standards finalized, they must design, develop and market phones with 5G radios in a market where more than 4 billion smartphones are in circulation globally. Even as 5G smartphones get shipped, it will take years before they are post-mainstream and pervasive.

The other main barrier to 5G adoption rests in mobile carrier network infrastructure – aka cell towers. The spacing of current towers accommodates cell phones that could easily connect from a 40-mile radius. However, the low-millimeter wavelength used by 5G phones, while increasing spectrum availability and data speeds, has a much lower range and cannot pass through thicker obstructions. Covering 3G/4G cell tower-equivalent range means 5G installations require microcells and the corresponding mobile backhaul_(where wired connectivity meets air connectivity), which increases the cost and complexity of network deployment.

No discussion of 5G is complete without alluding to its geopolitical significance. As *TIME* magazine recently said, "5G means a lot more than just another bar on your cell phone." There is an all-out cold war going on between the U.S., its allies and China. Chinese mobile giant Huawei has the early lead, cornering most of the market, but the U.S. and many European countries are taking steps to mitigate its advance. The stakes are high because losing this cold war "could slow down or dramatically alter the rollout of a technology that is likely to define the future of the Internet."

Lastly, understand that while 5G is a space race, we're still firmly in a 4G market. Hardware and regulatory environments are still playing catch-up. When they do catch up, we can say with certainty that patent holders for 5G standards will be the winners, harkening back to firms that provided jeans and shovels to cash in on the California Gold Rush in the early 20th century.

If connectivity's fast and steady march has made inroads to the previous building blocks we've examined, it has fully paved the way for the last one – sensing.

1.5 Sensing:
The Story of Deeper Data and Greater Acuity

Let's return to the scene set while exploring storage, our first building block. Don Draper, the *Mad Men* lead and creative genius, steps off the elevator, enters his advertising agency's hallway, turns the corner and witnesses the IBM System/360. Massive. Beastly. Loud. Within it rests the embryonic forces of digital that have accelerated, miniaturized and become accessible to the masses. And here we catch the first glimpse of sensing.

Sensing is simply detection and response to a stimulus from a physical environment. Sensors are the components that do the sensing.

Compared to the multiplicity of sensors on today's digital devices, sensing in the 1960s was relatively Jurassic. The IBM and its mainframe counterparts used a sensor known as a punch card. A long, rigid and thick piece of card stock most often the color of a manila folder, the punch card input data through a series of square holes populating 12 rows and 80 columns. Punch cards carried data input, offered data output and were also a very primitive, low-level storage solution.

While generally obsolete, they enjoyed a resurgence in the 2000 presidential election between George W. Bush and Al Gore. Perhaps you remember the "hanging chad" incident that called into question votes in Florida? That approach to voting leveraged punch cards working with a system that tallied votes.

By 1990, the mouse and keyboard had primarily replaced the punch card. These sensors offered a way to input – and witness the output of – data.

As with previous chapters, we ultimately see the most striking impact of a building block when we begin examining a smartphone. Smartphones carry the highest concentration of sensors on a digital device outside a Mars rover and underscore a distinction between two types of sensing: explicit and implicit. Explicit sensors, as the name suggests, are in the foreground of user experience. Punch cards, keyboards and "mice" are examples of explicit sensors. The smartphone carries an array of explicit sensors that include:

A touch screen for navigating the entirety of the device.

Fingerprint identification for locking and unlocking the device.

At least two cameras for recording video and taking still images away from and toward the user.

Up to four microphones for voice communication.

GPS for navigation and personalized search.

Iris ID, another form of biometric identification and security leveraging the iris of the eye.

Facial recognition, the most advanced form of biometric identification and security.

Smartphones also include implicit sensors. Rarely user accessed, implicit sensors most often function in the background, keeping the phone working and functional. These include:

Ambient light of the touch screen and a flash that doubles as a flashlight.

A compass for gauging direction.

Proximity location for powering the user experience and tracking a phone.

An accelerometer to measure the phone's proximity in motion that often works in sync with GPS for gauging estimated times of arrival.

A gyroscope that can sense the phone's position – commonly experienced when the screen rotates automatically from landscape to portrait.

A barometer to detect and measure pressure and enhance GPS performance in higher elevations where increased pressure can adversely impact results.

Up to three water sensors to alert users and technical support to water infiltration and/or diagnose water damage.

Sensing's trajectory rests in the volume of new and ever-increasing complexity and the sensitivity of the sensors themselves; this has gone from one to more than 20 automated, interactive, incredibly acute components designed for inputs, outputs and functionalities that are agile, flexible and powerful.

Consistent with previous building blocks, sensing's evolutionary path blends miniaturization and cost reduction at the intersection of increased complexity. Still and moving image photography drive this point home.

In 2005, Canon's PowerShot S2 IS was one of the most sophisticated consumer digital cameras on the market. Shaped like a traditional camera with an expanding lens and a flash, it would capture images at 5 megapixels of resolution. It weighed 1.12 pounds and cost $500.

Today's iPhone SE has a front-facing 7-megapixel camera and a rear-facing 12-megapixel camera. It can also shoot motion picture-quality 4K video footage. To that end, several films have leveraged the iPhone to do just that. In May 2019, Academy Award-winning director Claude Lelouche premiered *The Best Years of a Life* at the Cannes Film Festival. Portions were shot on an iPhone. The iPhone X weighs in at 3.99 ounces and costs as little as $399.

As we move into sensing's next phase, its variety will only continue to multiply and evolve with speed and sophistication. As IoT grows and converges with AI, sensing will grow with it in significance and acuity. Whether it's gauging water quality or imbedded in AI technologies making decisions and acting in human ways, its role is expanding. By 2022, Allied Market Research (AMR) predicts, the sensor market will grow to $241 billion.

1.6 The Machine in Full:
The Five Building Blocks and LOAR

With each building block, we've painted a picture of innovation marked by expansion, miniaturization, acceleration and cost reduction that lead to increased power and capability, mass production, mass accessibility, mass adoption and more diversified markets and revenue streams.

In some respects, looking at each building block in isolation seems a purely academic exercise. We've located each one in history and tracked its evolution. We've surveyed the present-day landscape on the basis of current trends. But there is a logic in this approach with a critical payoff.

When we move from silos on the ground to the big picture of a fully intelligent machine, we can begin to ask: What happens when they build simultaneously, one on top of the other?

To illustrate, let's explore the cumulative consumer impact of the building blocks by benchmarking advances in the iPhone over time. The following is a comparison between the iPhone 3G released in 2008 and the iPhone 8 released in 2017:

Device storage moved from 16 MB to 256 MB, representing a 16x increase.

Computing power shifted from 412 MHz to 2.4 GHz, representing a 6x increase.

Software, measured in apps available in the Apple Store, went from 85,000 to 2.2 million, representing a 26x increase.

Cellular connectivity speeds jumped from 54 Mbps to 1 Gpbs, representing a 20x increase.

Total installed sensors grew from 8 to 19, representing a 2x increase.

Ask yourself: What is the best way to understand the cumulative consumer impact, when each of the building blocks has shown impressive growth?

Is it one foot in front of the other? Is the speed determined *by the increase in the slowest advancing building block*, which is thereby the impact of the total machine? It's not unlike the slow and steady innovation in a chemical factory and would suggest that the overall consumer impact is something like 2x.

Is it instead additive? Does it mean that the addition of the increases in each building block renders the impact of the total machine? Slightly faster than the chemical factory, it's comparable to the difference between accomplishing something solo versus working on a team at the speed of daily life and would suggest that the total consumer impact is something like 62x.

Or is it multiplicative? Does each building block grow with relentless aggression and a seemingly inexplicable speed that is correlative to the impact of the total machine? More akin to cosmic expansion, it would suggest that the full consumer impact hits an astounding range – somewhere between 1,000x and 10,000x territory.

As you think about that, let's explore whether the cumulative consumer impact, and the implied rate of corporate growth, can be compared to market capitalization. Doing so begins to paint a bigger picture in a different context.

In 1995, the top 10 companies by market capitalization were long-haul, established businesses that had built their totals over more than a half-century. They included juggernauts such as Royal Dutch Shell, GE, Exxon Mobil, Toyota, Coca-Cola and Walmart.

Also in 1995? There was no Google. In 2004? There was no Facebook. At the beginning of 2009? There was no Uber. In 2015? There was no TikTok. Yet now, each company, just two decades later, holds a higher market cap than any one of the top 10 in 1995. Becoming so big so fast means they were able to deliver premium value to customers in a blink. It also indicates multiplicative – and not "one foot" or additive – impact.

This example foreshadows an answer to the question about speed in innovation that preceded it. Digital's multiplicative journey to date raises another critical question: How long can that journey last?

For that, we turn to Raymond Kurzweil, an MIT educated inventor and futurist. He's written extensively on health, artificial intelligence and transhumanism. Transhumanism is a philosophical approach that encourages the use of technology to transform the human condition by enhancing our intellectual capability and physiology. In 1999 he received the National Medal of Technology and Innovation from President Bill Clinton – America's highest technological honor.

Kurzweil built a theory that begins to explain the quickening of innovation across the five digital building blocks and technology as a whole. He calls it the Law of Accelerating Returns (LOAR). LOAR looks at technological advancement not as a series of linear events. Instead, it sees them as a cumulative exponential advancement through time. So thorough is this advancement that it impacts the rate of progress itself.

"So, we won't experience 100 years of progress in the 21st century – it will be more like 20,000 years of progress (at today's rate). The 'returns,' such as chip speed and cost-effectiveness, also increase exponentially. There's even exponential growth in the rate of exponential growth," Kurzweil said. "Within a few decades, machine intelligence will surpass human intelligence, leading to The Singularity – technological change so rapid and profound it represents a rupture in the fabric of human history. The implications include the merger of biological and nonbiological intelligence, immortal software-based humans, and ultra-high levels of intelligence that expand outward in the universe at the speed of light."

As you take in Kurzweil, remember, he's a futurist. There is a prophetic aspect to his words that might not ring true. At the same time, it gives texture to the rate at which the forces we've examined advance. They don't grow at the speed of ordinary time. They don't grow in an additive fashion. Their rate of growth is multiplying. Exponentially. All the time.

It's not unlike the moment when the Hubble Space Telescope began to beam back images of the billions of galaxies that dot the universe. The realizations that emerge from such a veil pulled back can leave us awestruck and humbled.

By applying these five building blocks to the new technologies they are producing, we can only expect the awe and humility to deepen. That's where we go next in Part 2.

Part 2
The Machine in Action

So far, we've thoroughly toured the intelligent machine. We defined and explored each of the machine's building blocks, tracing its history, teasing out ground-level innovations and unfolding the multiplicative impact of all five building blocks – storage, computing, software, connecting and sensing – stacked upon the other.

Now it's time to pull out from the machine itself to watch it in action, tracking seven powerful ways in which digital innovation has woven itself into society and business:

Big Data

The Cloud

Cybersecurity

Artificial intelligence

Augmented and virtual reality

Digital currencies

The post-screen IoT world

Along the way, we will snapshot the power of digital to change forever the ways we think, conduct business and go about our daily lives. If Part 1 has given us the grounding we need to understand digital, Part 2 will enable us to build the framework we need for recognizing, analyzing and seizing opportunities in digital.

2.1 Big Data:
The New Oil

As a resource, oil dates back to the fourth century when China tapped the first wells to fuel lamps and facilitate processes in ancient construction. Its modern history is traced to the mid-19th century, when a Scottish chemist, James Young, noticed a thin liquid seeping in the depths of a coal mine. He distilled samples and discovered that, as a thinned liquid, it could maintain a flame for lanterns and, in its thicker form, it proved appropriate for lubrication. Along with geologist Edward Binney, Young formed a collaboration that resulted in the first modern-day oil refinery that leveraged coal and output commercialized oil and paraffin wax. Around the same time, Canadian geologist Abraham Pineo Gesner found that liquid from coal, shale and bitumen could be refined into a cheaper, purer lamp oil that he called kerosene. As the industrial revolution ended, the petroleum revolution began.

John D. Rockefeller, the world's first bona fide oil baron, started Standard Oil Co. in 1865, the forerunner to today's ExxonMobil. Standard accounted for approximately 90% of America's refining capacity while simultaneously dominating the parts and machinery supply chain required to obtain it. At the turn of the century, oil was also discovered in Iran by William Knox D'Arcy, founder of the Anglo-Persian Oil Co. (APOC), a precursor to British Petroleum (BP). The British government purchased 51% of the company seven years later to keep its navy afloat during World War I.

In the 20th century, the oil industry expanded again as production shifted from countries such as the U.S. and the United Kingdom, which produced oil solely to consume it, to countries that could build reserves surpassing their national needs. In 1960, this shift catalyzed a partnership between Iran, Iraq, Kuwait, Saudi Arabia and Venezuela to birth the Organization of Petroleum Exporting Countries (OPEC), which today counts 15 countries on its roster. Big Oil had emerged. Even in the face of climate change and having endured roller-coaster markets, oil remains a constant giant and, according to *Offshore Technology*, "it's thriving despite competition from renewable sources."

To what do we owe oil's ongoing significance within the global economy? First, it is core to countless industries, especially within the automotive, aviation and industrial sectors. Second, oil is a commodity that has no direct substitutes matching its scale. It powers and lubricates the global economy.

Recorded data – what we might call Small Data - predates the first oil well. More than 7,000 years ago, accounting was used in Mesopotamia, generating data for tracking and controlling the agricultural industry. Predictably, accounting underwent innovation. All sorts of useful and exciting information emerged, such as mortality rates, censuses, meteorological measurements over time and my favorite: statistics and records for the sport of cricket.

Big Data, the evolution of Small Data, is the new oil. It is a core reality of the expanding digital frontier. It forms a mammoth collection of diverse information that can be observed, analyzed and synthesized with velocity to discern patterns, trends and associations.

In 2005, the term Big Data solidified. At that time, it referred to a set of data so massive that existing intelligent machines couldn't process it. As data volume was exploding, technologists began Big Data projects to fast-track its sorting and analysis. An industry was born. In 2017, IBM announced that 80% of the world's total data originated in the previous two years. IDC projected that we would create 163 zettabytes (1 zettabyte = trillion GB) of data annually by 2026 – an almost unfathomable collection of data.

Technology companies such as Amazon (e-commerce, cloud), Facebook (social, chat), Google (search, browser, cloud), Apple (iOS, apps) and Microsoft (office applications, cloud) are responsible for the majority of this total. As we'll find out later, this is a key to understanding Big Data as the new oil. Each company can extract data from unrivaled interactivity by millions of users. Each company applies superior digital technology that has made it a de facto leader in advancing Big Data. Together, all five companies will continue to consolidate Big Data ownership in their favor over the short term.

Big Data & The Big Five

Amazon, Facebook, Google, Apple and Microsoft are not only drilling for their own online data, they're seizing opportunities to blend it with offline data. Even today, in the United States, 90% of retail and 70% of daily life happens offline.

Because of this, the first consideration these giants are sizing up and seizing exists in the offline world of data that only serves to deepen their dominance online. They can afford to buy offline data from third parties, "mash it up" with their own and other third-party-purchased online data and gain a 360-degree window into consumer behavior and activities. This data equips them to precision target and tailor content, advertising and sales while refining the user experience. It also continually greases the skids of monetization.

In 2017, Niraj Dawar penned a *Harvard Business Review* article making the case that Google had proven its online ads could trigger purchases in brick and mortar environments. That's because Google could link the ads it served to credit and debit card transaction data it had purchased from third parties, closing the loop on consumer behavior. Dewar contended Google's move countered a Facebook initiative to track consumer store visits and similar transactions through third-party partnerships with Square and Marketo. This ability to acquire and blend data in ways that impact consumer behavior accounts for why 70% of 2019's total digital ad spend went to Google, Facebook and Amazon.

The second consideration we must hold is that all five companies are using powerful technology to drive real time insights from large amounts of unstructured data. Unstructured data is not the neatly organized stuff of an Excel spreadsheet or some other table or common identifier. It is either semi-structured (e.g., social media posts) or unstructured (e.g., text, video and image files). The ability to seize and make unstructured data useful is of incredible competitive advantage, but it can only be leveraged by major technology players who have the know-how to process it.

Rob Kitchin in *The Data Revolution: Big Data, Open Data, Data Infrastructures and Their Consequences* describes unstructured data as not having "a defined data model or common identifiable structure. Each element, such as narrative text or photo, may have a specific structure or format, but not all data within a dataset share the same structure. As such, while they can be searched and queried, they are not easily combined or computationally analyzed [but] some estimates suggest that such data are growing at 15 times the rate of structured data."

Storing and analyzing exhaustive volumes of unstructured data requires sophisticated tools. Apache Hadoop is an app that tackles unstructured data by marshaling the computing power of many networks simultaneously. Artificial intelligence (AI) and machine learning (MLR) can perform with exponential effectiveness as they process more and more unstructured data sets. Amazon, Google, Facebook, Apple and Microsoft deploy these types of tools and, because they are creating massive datasets every hour, they hold a natural advantage in Big Data.

The final reason the Big Five hold natural superiority in the Big Data game rests in their ability to organize data around an individual. In the early days of the internet, there was a tongue-in-cheek adage about internet anonymity that went, "On the internet, nobody knows if you're a dog." It's no longer true. Most aspects of online and offline activity are organized around individuals, thus giving powerful insights to drive personalization and microtargeting. As a result, and just like regulatory moves around oil production and trade, increased government involvement in Big Data has ensued. A Federal Trade Commission study broke down the amount of information a data broker could mine around an individual:

"Data collected could include bankruptcy information, voting registration, consumer purchase data, web browsing activities, warranty registrations, and other details of consumers' everyday interactions," the study found. "While each data broker source may provide only a few data elements about a consumer's activities, data brokers can put all of these data elements together to form a more detailed composite of the consumer's life. For example, one of the nine data brokers had 3000 data segments for nearly every U.S. consumer."

While data drives big profits among a few major players, it's also recalibrating digital user expectations. If you've lived in a major metropolitan area with a profound car culture such as Los Angeles, Washington, D.C., or Chicago, you might remember how, back in the day, you needed a Thomas Guide to get anywhere. It was a thick, neighborhood by neighborhood atlas consisting of hundreds of pages of city streets and an elaborate key for matching a specific address to one of thousands of quadrants on individual maps.

Now we plug in an address to Google Maps even if we know it by heart just to gauge travel time and perhaps an alternate, faster route. Google's Big Data competence enables it to deliver an experience that matches the expectation. Data on distance is married to road construction data, public transportation data and real time traffic conditions. But we also want more. We want to know if there is a café en route, if it's open, if it has a drive-thru and how we can factor that into total travel time. Not only have we ditched our Thomas Guides, we demand full concierge services from Google Maps. Across industries, this type of base user expectation around getting real time, personalized recommendations through computational analytics is only rising.

Another company harnessing Big Data at the intersection of user experience is India-based Reliance JIO Platforms (JIO). Its focus? First-time-user experiences. The platform component of its name cues that it is doing a lot in digital, and we'll focus on one: mobile phones. JIO has driven the price for data and mobile phone hardware to industry lows. Last year it offered six months of free data for new subscribers. Over the previous four years, it attracted more than 400 million users. Its next goal is to connect the rest of India's 600 million people who are not yet using mobile devices. Tech companies – including Google, Facebook, Intel and Qualcomm – have invested more than $20 billion since March 2020. Google is working with JIO on a reconfigured version of Android that will pave the way for developing extremely low-cost, entry-level smartphones to speed adoption.

Google's Sundar Pichai reflected on the deal by saying, "Together we are excited to rethink, from the ground up, how millions of users in India can become owners of smartphones. This effort will unlock new opportunities, further power the vibrant ecosystem of applications and push innovation to drive growth for the new Indian economy."

At the deal's launch, Reliance Chairperson Mukesh Ambani outlined the full scope of JIO's digital vision:

"In the next three years, I can see a strong path for JIO to connect over half a billion mobile customers, over a billion smart sensors, and over 50 million homes and business establishments. ... JIOMart, in addition to grocery, will expand to cover electronics, fashion, pharmaceuticals, and healthcare in the days ahead [and] Jio Healthcare will provide end-to-end healthcare services," he said.

As it follows this path, JIO's strategy, particularly at the intersection of 5G and Big Data, is seen as the model by members of the U.S. Department of State's Bureau of Economic and Business Affairs. Robert L. Strayer, the bureau's deputy assistant secretary for cyber and international communications and information policy, underscored that JIO's move to create its own 5G solutions and its deployment of "trusted partners" (read: not Huawei) has led to a deepened trade relationship between India and the U.S. in a greater geopolitical game around 5G infrastructure at the intersection of Big Data.

JIO and the rest of the digital industry understand that only a small set of players can play this game, giving them a potentially insurmountable competitive advantage.

This brings us back to oil.

Like oil, Big Data has always "been in the ground." Big data reserves are growing exponentially by the minute. Since ancient history, civilizations have used both resources in novel ways. Like oil, data, when matched to technology akin to a modern refinery, has become the object of commercial interest and investigation. As the utility of both resources increased, both flowed in ways that fuel the economy. Because of this fact, oil and big data are commodities marked by inelastic demand: hunger for it remains high, no matter its price. Finally, because of the incredible amount of digital power and sophistication required to exploit its richness, data, like oil, is owned by an oligopolistic supply side. ExxonMobil, BP and Royal Dutch Shell? Meet Amazon, Google and Facebook.

Big Data is indeed the new oil. Much of it exists in the cloud, a significant application of digital technology that has transformed business and is reestablishing innovation and healthy tension between centralized and decentralized computing.

2.2 Cloud:
Digital Power from Afar

In Neil Postman's landmark book, *Technopoly*, he introduces how, in the 12th and 13th centuries, Benedictine monks sought to create a mechanical clock that could mark the seven periods of devotion throughout a day. Could they have imagined the multiplicative and unintended byproducts of their invention? The clock's ability to regiment hours of work, production and standardization paved the way for capitalism.

"The paradox, the surprise and the wonder are that the clock was invented by [people] who wanted to devote themselves more rigorously to God; it ended as the technology of greatest use to [people] who wished to devote themselves to the accumulation of money," Postman said.

Reading this and setting aside the sacred-secular implications of the example, you might sense that I'm equating the cloud to an elemental discovery or invention such as fire, the wheel, the internal combustion engine or the telephone. Or the clock. The cloud is not that glamorous. However, when people talk about the evolution of the internet and digital technology, it's easy to talk about life in terms of living "B.C." – Before Cloud. How is B.C. life best described? For business, it held significant inequities.

We mark the B.C. "epoch" somewhere between 1994 and 2006 – the infancy into preteen eras of e-commerce. It was a time when startups almost had to practice alchemy to anticipate demand for computing storage and server capacity. At the very least, they had to be thorough and lucky.

A late 1990s Super Bowl ad illustrated this aspect of B.C. life with precision. A small group working with an e-commerce startup huddles around a computer workstation in its hip, industrial workspace. The developer in the group presses a button, and the site goes live. The camera shifts to the screen and a sale appears, accompanied by a very digital, audible ding – everyone cheers. There is adulation. High-fives all around. Then there are more dings. And more. The team begins to gulp amid looks of confusion and despair. We cut back to the screen, and tens of thousands of orders climb like an altimeter. The team is crestfallen, and the implications are clear. The website server is going to crash. The team severely miscalculated infrastructure capacity. Triumph turned to tragedy in less than 15 seconds.

This 30-second spot served as a cautionary tale around how, when demand outstripped the server, the server would crash. The flip side that held equally disastrous implications was overestimating capacity – an "if you build it and they don't come" scenario. Lower demand resulted in wasted storage space that would tie up valuable capital. The level of unpredictability required companies – particularly small and even midsize startups – to do everything they could to prophesy demand and modulate website and product launches to mitigate catastrophic scaling or low to no traffic. They had to get it just right. It greatly impacted marketing. Soft launches might set radical expectations with investors around the limitations of technology and force a modulation of customer access. When launches rendered little traffic, startups desperately had to find a way to escalate visibility quickly and differentiate themselves to create demand and get their return on tech investment. It was a real problem.

It was also a conundrum that drove the inequality between life pre-cloud and post-cloud. In the B.C. era, large organizations with enterprise data centers held a competitive advantage – namely, the resources to manage server setup and scalability. Amazon was a case in point. It launched in 1994. In 1997 it went public. It was a hypergrowth startup.

In its first decade, Amazon touted itself as the world's largest bookstore and won people over with customer service and ease of use. Its end game was always to compete as a beyond-big-box retailer. To that end, in 1998, Amazon added toys and games. In the meantime, the company's back office was hard at work trying to solve this significant challenge of scalability, capacity and power. In the early 2000s, Amazon created the now well-documented APIs that enabled internal teams to access common infrastructure services. In 2006, the company leveled the playing field for all by offering the same service to third parties as the Amazon Elastic Compute Cloud, single-handedly ushering in the era of cloud computing. Importantly, by successfully navigating concerns around server setup and scalability, Amazon answered its critics and secured profitability.

Defined by research company Gartner Inc. as "scalable and elastic IT-related capabilities provided as a service to third parties over the internet," the Elastic Compute Cloud was an immediate hit. Business embraced it, figuring it into their infrastructure strategies. With the cloud, they not only had to invest much less capital and resources into a new project, they also had fewer operational problems compared to running in-house infrastructure. This move also impacted startup communities – from angel and Series A darlings to mom-and-pop solopreneurs. It revolutionized the amount of capital and infrastructure required to go to market.

The cloud also spawned a whole new economy of services. Beyond the initial "infrastructure as a service" or IaaS (renting storage, computing, firewall/security, networking), cloud providers developed "platform as a service," or PaaS (IaaS coupled with an operating system, database management, development tools and more). Then came "software as a service" or SaaS (software applications hosted over the internet). The public cloud infrastructure services market is expected to reach $132.5 billion worldwide in 2020.

Its growth extends beyond e-commerce, however, and you've undoubtedly experienced its power in your work and life, where it has proved transformative to personal computing. It might seem like the cloud, the great liberator, is a panacea. It's not, and even though the cloud sparked a revolution, not all B.C. era tools such as the enterprise data center are obsolete. The cloud has some real issues that prevent 100% migration.

Lack of security is one issue. Leading cloud providers have invested heavily to protect data and IP, touting protection for "data in transit" and "data at rest." Amazon Web Services offers more than 1,800 security control features, including Amazon Macie, a machine-learning service to "automatically discover, classify, and protect sensitive data on the Amazon S3 cloud." Similarly, Google offers the data loss prevention API for "fast, scalable classification and optional redaction for sensitive data elements like credit card numbers, names, social security numbers, passport numbers, U.S. and selected international driver's license numbers, and phone numbers."

These types of measures are not foolproof. The Pentagon recently learned this the hard way when 100 GB of U.S. Army and NSA intelligence data leaked on its public cloud. Organizations are understandably skittish of parking their critical systems, confidential data and intellectual property with someone else in a remote data center. In-house, co-located enterprise data centers offer comfort and security.

It's also important to note that as of now, total migration to the cloud is hard, if not impossible. Moving workloads from enterprise data centers proves costly and complicated, primarily when the organization must deal with its legacy systems. Strategically, more substantial companies may see such a move as eroding their ability to control data. Cloud Architect Jo Harder likens the decision to one of buying vs. renting a condo.

"Much like living within the confines of a building owned by someone else, it may not be possible to host workloads in the same way as your own environment," Harder said. "While it is likely that the cloud offers new and better options for security, monitoring, and analytics, there may also be some unexpected limitations based on the inherent multi-tenancy associated with cloud. Further, some level of control is relinquished when renting a virtual cloud condo."

A definitive solution to both the security and control-meets-legacy issue foregrounds why total migration to public cloud is not currently feasible. This fact has given rise to the hybrid cloud. As its name suggests, it blends an on-site private cloud and third-party, public cloud services. The two platforms fulfill blended roles. Hybrid cloud configurations usually leverage on-site enterprise data centers that handle key applications and steady computing workloads and deploy one or more public clouds for fast-growing or high-variability demand. This best-of-both-worlds solution maintains existing in-house data centers and expertise while exploiting the newest cloud technologies.

Hybrid clouds are increasingly popular and particularly well suited for a specific company or industry needs. *ZDNet* illustrated how hybrid clouds are a terrific fit for trading floors, reporting that "pushing trade orders through the private cloud infrastructure and running analytics on trades from the public cloud infrastructure greatly decreases the amount of physical space needed for the latency-sensitive task of making trade orders."

This approach checks the data security box and leaves control around threshold-defined trading algorithms in the hands of the investment firms that have built their models around them. The hybrid model dramatically reduces risk exposure that could, in a worst-case scenario, end their businesses.

Issues of risk management and strategy serve as roadblocks to total cloud. The cloud also carries some technical baggage that has proved problematic to digital evolution. These issues merit a more in-depth examination. We'll explore them through a specific innovation designed to solve many of the cloud's technical problems: edge computing.

Edge Computing

Edge is best understood if we turn our attention to computing architecture. Architectural philosophy and technology have traveled a continuum between centralization and decentralization. In the B.C. era, computing happened on giant mainframes in large organizations – it was centralized, and the hardware just sat there. Personal computers and the "client-server" framework of the early 1980s meant that computing became decentralized – they were more portable and, in the advent of the internet, leveraged in lots of new places outside an enterprise. Smartphones and mobile applications further decentralized architecture as they have become practical extensions of the hand and powerful touchpoints for productivity.

Paradoxically, cloud computing has reversed this process. Public cloud providers such as Amazon, Google, Alibaba, Microsoft and

IBM have re-centralized in mega data centers. Built on vast swaths of property sometimes in rather remote areas, these data centers illustrate how successful the cloud has become.

As engineers began getting inside the cloud and concurrently innovating digital, cloud performance and application began posing several challenges. The pendulum started swinging back toward architectural decentralization. As novel uses of the cloud have driven new technologies that leverage it, several aspects of cloud interaction have proven problematic. The potentially biggest and first problem is latency.

We've all experienced latency. In cloud environments, it's the delay between requests made on our digital device and the response time of the cloud provider. More thoroughly, it is the time required to transmit digital device sensor data to the cloud and the total time for the cloud to analyze and retransmit data with the necessary instructions to execute what happens next. You've experienced it if you've ever browsed the web and clicked through to a new site. If the website doesn't load immediately, that's latency. For the website's owner, the implications have consequences. Websites that take 0.5 seconds to load on a browser experience a 20% drop in users. Now consider this aggravation in more advanced contexts.

When constant, near-instantaneous analyses and decision-making in the cloud are a must, latency can endanger its viability. Digital voice assistants that don't respond or a paused experience of virtual reality can threaten adoption. Autonomous vehicles needing to swerve out of harm's way or a time-critical suture in robotic surgery can imperil lives.

A second major challenge of cloud computing is bandwidth. Even though network bandwidth has increased with the advent of 5G, a massive uptick in how many devices connect at once (the Internet of Things, or IoT) will start generating ever-larger amounts of data and clogging the system. According to a report by IDC, 41.6 billion IoT devices will generate 79.4 zettabytes of data (remember, 1 zettabyte = 1,000,000,000,000,000,000,000 bytes) by 2025, and this growth will continue unabated. Transmitting this much data for cloud-based, centralized computing adds data management costs to cloud and enterprise data centers. It's architecturally inefficient.

The third concern around cloud computing rests in three sacred and reputation-risking factors: privacy, security and data's regulatory landscape. Transferring all data to the cloud becomes dicey when personally identifiable information (PII) such as Social Security numbers and biometrics are involved. It's simply not as secure. This risk prompted Apple to store user fingerprints and facial recognition coordinates in a secure enclave within the iPhone itself. Apple has publicly reinforced this move by explicitly announcing that this type of data is never stored on its servers or backed up via iCloud – again, it's not secure enough for this type of unique, one-of-kind personal information.

The cloud's final challenge rests in a simple question: What if it goes down? In 2018, during a mega-outage at Amazon Web Services (AWS), dozens of AWS-hosted consumer applications, including Expedia, GitHub and Flipboard, were unavailable for hours at a time. Here are a representative array of outages in 2019: Amazon AWS (two in a row!), Salesforce, Apple iCloud, Microsoft, Google Cloud Servers, Google Cloud Platform, Cloudflare, Facebook and Instagram (together). Outages are pervasive and catastrophic. Most businesses want end-user devices and applications to be functionally active, even when internet connectivity is intermittent.

Edge computing addresses this entire bundle of problems. Instead of the cloud method, where data computes at one or many mega data centers, edge computing takes place at or near the data source.

Computing moves from the "center" (either the cloud or an enterprise data center) to the "edge" (e.g., smartphones, drones, autonomous cars, robots or any other intelligent machine tethered to the internet).

Edge is gaining traction. According to Gartner, today only 10% of data is processed outside data centers or the cloud. By 2022, 75%, of data and more than 50% of companies, will spend more of their IT budgets on storage, networks and computing in edge locations versus their own data centers.

Gartner also anticipates that edge computing adoption will fuel the annual growth of decentralized computing by 35% to $6.7 billion. Its deployment will open up, differentiate and disrupt several markets. We've already discussed autonomous vehicles, where contextual data needs to be collected and analyzed quickly, and augmented and virtual reality devices, which can prevent motion sickness for users by minimizing data transmission latency. It will also prove critical to industrial automation, where sensors can quickly analyze and act on ambient signals, and sensor-based remote inspections in agriculture and other appropriate, inspection-requisite industries.

As leading players in AI (artificial intelligence), the topic of our next chapter, bring machine learning to the edge, growth will ensue. In 2019, Google launched Edge TPU, which facilitates lightning-fast machine learning in mobile devices using edge computing. Imagine real time speech recognition and response, being able to sort and classify thousands of images at once and authentically full-scale automated CRM – all made possible by "the edge." These types of innovation have led Dell CEO and founder Michael Dell to assert that "Edge computing could be 100 times bigger than the Internet as we know it today. That may sound crazy right now, but give it a few years, and I think that will be more understood."

Over the long haul, edge computing likely will coexist with public and private clouds. Decisioning will depend on prioritizing latency, privacy, convenience and bandwidth. Either way, it is offering new ways to sate the need for computing speed.

As we've witnessed across this chapter, cloud computing is a tremendous achievement. Following the "B.C." era, the cloud-enabled digital world equipped small companies to innovate and compete with large organizations. "The new" doesn't always displace "the old," and this has brought the cloud down to earth. Enterprise data centers still have a lot to offer and are not becoming extinct anytime soon. Greater coexistence with cloud technologies may be the next evolutionary step!

Whether in the cloud or at the edge, we now move to a byproduct of all digital technologies: challenges that require increasingly vigilant cybersecurity.

2.3 Cybersecurity:
Threats, Protection and Response

You're watching a spy movie from the mid-20th century. An international person of intrigue is trying to get the diamonds from a mansion somewhere in Monte Carlo. She needs to find ways around the security guards. Ingeniously, someone has brought a phone that she wires into existing telecommunications lines from a strangely well-lit tunnel within sight of the house. There's a close-up of a finger dialing – the old school way to input a number. On the other end, a phone's bell rings and the receiver lifts to a face. We back out to a long shot. It's the head of security, whose swiveling office chair turns from his security video monitors. There is a long silence. "Hello?" The call hangs up even as we see an array of thieves in black tights smoothly choreograph an entrance in the monitors as the confused security guard shakes his head.

Imagine this same kind of scenario in a digital environment, and multiply it daily to the power of 10. It begins to reveal the frequency and methodology of cyberattacks. More than likely, you've experienced one. If a computer virus has ever plagued you, or you've had a go-to website taken down by a cyberattack or even worse, if you've had fraudulent activity on your credit card, you know that cybersecurity is no joke. Cyberthreats – their frequency, diversity and sophistication – steadily escalate, threatening individuals, corporations and governments. Over just the last year, here are some of the attacks levied in both experimental and real-world contexts:

Attendees of the Black Hat Briefings conference, an annual gathering of hackers, government agencies and corporations focused on cybersecurity, watched researchers overcome the Apple iPhone's Face ID in 120 seconds. They used a combination of eyeglasses, tape and the face of a sleeping/unconscious iPhone user.

A vulnerability discovered in Google Camera's app allowed a hacker to gain control of the camera and take still images, record video and audio of conversations and identify the user's whereabouts – all without the user's realizing the app was highjacked.

Windows users across all varieties – from Windows XP to 10 – were left exposed to such a degree that Microsoft, the National Security Agency (NSA) and the U.S. Department of Homeland Security's Cybersecurity and Infrastructure Security Agency (CISA) loudly announced software update requirements. The vulnerability known as BlueKeep would render devices inoperable while focusing impact on the operating system's Remote Desktop Protocol, which enables remote individual device control to move documents, snag updates and undergo troubleshooting or repairs online. It enabled BlueKeep's ferocious spread.

The city of New Orleans proclaimed a state of emergency as its systems and network were taken down by a ransomware attack: Hackers took the city's entire network and systems down in expectation of getting paid a ransom. New Orleans chose not to pay, implemented a disaster recovery plan and was back online within four days. It cost $7 million. The city's cyber insurance policy covered only $3 million.

More than 5,000 data breaches occurred, compromising more than 7 billion users' personal data. Some brands impacted by the attacks included Capital One, State Farm and Sprint.

The diversity and complexity of these examples spotlight why cybersecurity is one of the most vital considerations in digital strategies. It embodies the technologies and processes designed to protect computers, devices, systems, networks and data from vulnerabilities, threats and unauthorized access. To fully explore it requires understanding key terms and lingo around some common forms of attack.

Cybersecurity serves as the first line of defense against many common threats. Phishing is a social engineering scam used to get sensitive data, often using a combination of email and a fake replica website such as a financial institution. Malware is software that can gain access, steal data, extort and execute diverse forms of harm. Intrusion constitutes overcoming a weak password or exploiting a weakness within operating systems. Unencrypted or unsecured data is information sitting exposed to potential destruction or theft. Denial of service is a cyberattack that drives out real internet traffic through the introduction of "bad" traffic that can take down whole systems. Moreover, cybersecurity must react decisively to minimize damage when attacks succeed.

To keep the challenges and opportunities of cybersecurity simple, we will explore three considerations. First, we'll ground ourselves in data breaches and why they happen. Next, we'll deepen understanding around how the intelligent machine can carry inherent breach risk within a key building block. Finally, we'll examine blockchain, an innovation that is strengthening cybersecurity across the globe.

Data Breaches

The Identity Theft Resource Center (ITRC) defines a data breach as "an incident in which an individual name plus a Social Security number, driver's license number, medical record or financial record (credit/debit cards included) is potentially put at risk because of exposure."

As reflected above, data breaches happen all the time. It's not a matter of if; it's a matter of when. And often it can also be a matter of "whom." The 2017 data breach at Equifax is a case in point.

As a multinational consumer credit reporting agency and one of the three largest agencies of its type in the world, the Equifax data breach created instant visceral headlines. Equifax was a perceived leader in cybersecurity because it warehouses some of the world's most private personal data on nearly anyone who holds a credit history.

Forbes detailed the breach, reporting that "an authorized third party gained access to Equifax data on as many as 143 million Americans. Included among files accessed by hackers was a treasure trove of personal data: names, dates of birth, Social Security numbers, addresses." Perhaps most painfully, hackers gained access because Equifax failed to patch one of its internet servers against what was a known, pervasive software flaw.

Never before had so much super-private data undergone such deep attack so publicly, making it one of the most serious in history. Equifax continues to repair its reputation and damage to its systems while navigating court costs and settlements. It reached a deal totaling more than $380 million in payouts to consumers. In 2019, it reached a separate $575 million agreement with the Federal Trade Commission, the Consumer Financial Protection Bureau and state attorneys general. As of this writing, Equifax had recently lost an attempt to get a suit dropped under the state of New York's "deceptive acts and practices law," paving the way for more damages.

The dramatic escalation in data breaches underscores a lack of cybersecurity savvy on the part of corporations and governments. While some incidents carry a level of technical complexity that are nuanced, most – such as Equifax's – happen because of a lack of vigilance around overdue software patches, poor access control, procedural misses and known application vulnerabilities. Large-scale data breaches happen in four common ways. Through a deceptive act, users or devices surrender a password account access. By exploiting weak access control, data gets stolen. In sizing up technical and architectural vulnerabilities, intrusion happens. Through discovering and surmounting of weak third-party access points to corporate systems, serious attacks of dramatic scope ensue. We'll now consider these methodologies in depth.

"Deceptive surrender" attacks require a level of digital social engineering. As an individual, perhaps you've experienced some type of scam that attempts to harvest your account information. These types of threats usually come in one of three flavors: phishing, spamming or spyware. Earlier, we discussed phishing. It often leverages bogus email or text alerts that take you to a replica website of, say, your financial institution, where you enter your login to see what's up.

Similarly, spamming may use what looks like a fully functional storefront wherein you enter your information connected to a good or service. Spyware might be a simple click-through of a faux URL that downloads unseen software that tracks keystrokes, analyzes them and sends them to a hacker. Most popular in mass individual account attacks, these approaches can be leveraged within corporate environments. They account for more than 50% of all breaches.

Yahoo! experienced this in 2016. At the time, it represented the single-largest data breach ever reported. A detailed postmortem by the FBI revealed that intrusion began with a "spear-phishing" email to an unsuspecting Yahoo! employee with system-level access. Once the hackers – also referred to as "state-sponsored actors" in this breach – got access to the system, they were able to impersonate actual account users through "forged cookies." Cookies are data stored in browsers to shortcut communication and personalize user experiences. This approach gave entrée, and hackers harvested names, addresses, telephone numbers, dates of birth, encrypted passwords and unencrypted security questions of more than 1.5 billion users.

Hackers also often prowl around where data is stored and transferred, looking for "weak access control." At the corporate level, risks emerge across an array of factors. Firms that leverage agile workforces that are tending towards BYOD (bring your own device) work environments offer a case in point. Many of the "own devices" do not have recommended mobile security solutions that, when interfacing with corporate networks and systems, create weaknesses, especially if paired with an unencrypted or low encryption network. WiFi networks that don't deploy high levels of encryption such as WEP, WPA or WPA2 creates opportunities for man in the middle (MITM) attacks wherein a hacker can drop into the signal to eavesdrop, steal information, corrupt data or sabotage communications.

Sometimes, however, companies simply don't encrypt their files. That's what happened to Anthem Inc., a health insurance giant fronted by brands such as Blue Cross Blue Shield, Amerigroup and Anthem Healthcare. In 2014, employees began noticing unusual queries into the Anthem database and brought in investigators. The source was found a year later, but not before 80 million Americans had their full names, addresses, Social Security numbers, birthdates, insurance membership numbers, medical IDs, employment information and income data stolen. A simple step – file encryption – could have prevented the largest health care hack in history.

"Technical and architectural vulnerabilities" result in sophisticated intrusions wherein hardware and software defenses are unforeseen or haven't yet caught up to hacker aggression. Zero-day attacks reflect such vulnerabilities. Through them, hackers unleash malware on a system before a developer can patch the weakness – thus the name "zero-day." However, most attacks are due to long-standing gaps or a lack of prudent security behaviors on the part of organizations.

Sony Pictures was the victim of a hack that found a weakness in its IT architecture that resulted in the release of confidential and proprietary information such as Sony's future releases, scripts under consideration and private emails between executives. There was also an attempt to erase the whole of Sony's computer infrastructure. A hacker group known as the Guardians of Peace took credit for the attack. It demanded that Sony not release a comedy that depicted the assassination of North Korean leader Kim Jong Un. U.S. intelligence officials alleged that North Korea was behind the attacks.

JPMorgan Chase fell victim to the single most massive theft of customer data of any financial institution in history because of technical weakness. Like most leading banks, JPMorgan Chase uses two-factor authentication (2FA) to enable employee access to its servers. This form of security means that once a correct password gets entered into a login, the user receives a text message with a code to double-check identity. It's a second simple yet effective layer of security.

However, JPMorgan Chase's security team forgot to install 2FA on one of its servers that, once discovered by hackers, enabled an easily breached point of entry to 90 additional servers. Hackers stole account information from more than 83 million households and small businesses.

Even if a company sufficiently secures its software systems, "weak third-party access points" to the company can create overall vulnerability.

Target experienced this type of attack. The company had provided an HVAC contractor with remote network access to facilitate vendor electronic billing and project management. Hackers compromised the HVAC firm's system, gained access to Target systems and installed credit card stealing malware at the cash registers within Target stores. The compromise of financial details surrounding 70 million customers and 40 million credit cards happened within two weeks. So pervasive was the attack that even after Target thought it had fully re-secured the system, a final diagnostic revealed malware still present on 25 registers.

Data breaches are increasing in both frequency and severity, and, for anyone serious about digital, precautions matter. Individually, there needs to be a high level of security literacy brought to bear – from maintaining strong, unique passwords and activating 2FA wherever it's available to frequently checking bank balances, backing up data and avoiding insecure WiFi networks.

For corporations, the FTC has published a detailed guide for a business response to data breaches at FTC.gov. It offers a solid initiation into incident preparation and response. Depending on the nature of your industry, hiring a dedicated chief security officer or creating a cybersecurity team to oversee physical and digital security is a best practice. Dovetailing that practice with a communications team will shore up the reputation management side of any incident.

Response timing is crucial. Cybersecurity firms consistently tout their speed of response following breach incidents for a good reason. *Security Week's* Wade Williamson details the typical sequence of steps from a data breach to monetization and makes a case for quick disclosure and rapid response. Attackers sell stolen data to brokers. Brokers sell cards, in batches, to individual criminals who use them to buy goods and services. Says Williams:

"As soon as it becomes apparent that a specific merchant has been compromised, all of the compromised cards will be quickly deactivated. This means that freshly stolen and active cards are highly valuable ($100 or more), while older cards can be worth pennies. This is a serious spread, and criminals need to know which sorts of cards they are buying, and the state of the cards they are holding. To address this challenge, criminals will periodically test a subset of their cards by using them to make small online purchases [and] quickly determine the percentage of cards that are active and working."

Breach Risks Inside the Intelligent Machine: Chips & Security

Sometimes the speed of innovation itself – and corporate battles for brand superiority – can leave intelligent machines vulnerable. One such flaw emerged from the development of chips. Earlier, as we toured the computing prowess of the intelligent machine, we discussed the evolution of chip size and velocity in ways that have advanced computing. In 2018, a data breach risk from not just one but two chip design flaws emerged that was breathtaking in its proportions.

As *CNNTech* reported, chip design flaws could "allow an attacker to read sensitive data stored in the memory, like a password." It also stated that every form of digital device, including desktops, laptops, smartphones and cloud servers, were affected by two bugs known as the Spectre and Meltdown.

"We have verified [the Spectre bug] on Intel, AMD, and ARM processors [and the] Meltdown appears to be specific to Intel Chips [from as far back as those released in 1995]."

It meant that such defects could have impacted every aspect of the internet. It also served as a cautionary tale. Tech companies go to great lengths to reassure us that our data is safe. Yet, in this case, hackers could have been stealing personal data over the last 20 years without anyone's knowing.

How could this happen? By this point, you roughly know how a CPU works. As it processes binary data, information that is not immediately needed is stored *away* from the CPU, in what we call storage. Information that requires immediacy is stored *close* to the CPU in what is known as memory. At the core of a computer's operating system is the kernel, a program that securely manages data coordination across apps, computing, storage and sensors. On the basis of what's needed, the kernel retrieves memory data, while ensuring data across apps is isolated or is accessible only after checking its access privilege. If you check your email and browse through Facebook on your smartphone simultaneously, memory data for your Facebook login is kept separate from your mail credentials.

As CPUs became insanely fast, the speed at which the kernel retrieved information became critical. The race was on, and chip manufacturers put a premium on speed. It resulted in an innovation known as "speculative execution," the performance of a task before it was needed, ensuring the preservation of time usually lost to information retrieval.

While this undoubtedly improved speed, it also created an opportunity for a malicious program to access memory that it should not have been able to read. Google's Project Zero team detailed three variants of problems coming from speculative execution – Spectre and Meltdown, alluded to above.

Hackers could use both Meltdown and Spectre to get access to sensitive data – logins, passwords, credit cards, banking records, financial data – that's used in memory by other applications. Meltdown, so-called because it effectively "melts down" basic security between programs, can be a real problem for cloud providers such as Amazon Web Services, where different clients use the same server. Spectre tricks programs into conducting random operations and leaving confidential information in the computer's memory, and the information can then be stolen.

Jake Swearingen broke it down in *New York Magazine.*

"If Meltdown allows you to crack open someone's diary and read it at will, Spectre is more akin to something that lets you flip open a random page in someone's diary and read one word at a time, and then flip to another random page and read one more word," he wrote. "It's not at all impossible to still get some very sensitive information, but it takes longer and requires more persistence."

As severe and pervasive as these chip defects are, a real fix through chip redesign could be a decade in the making.

Ultimately, security compromises are rife in the race to make computing as fast as possible. It puts the onus on the technology industry as a whole to find a better balance between innovating speed and security. It also requires intentional public/private partnerships to share security intelligence to realize a future of safe digital. There is hope. Google's Project Zero team, so named for dedication to stopping zero-day attacks and Google's public watchdog for all things cybersecurity, was among the first to discover the chip defects. Google then (privately) shared the info with Intel, Qualcomm, AMD, Microsoft and Apple. In turn, this "virtual consortium" leveraged a patch built by researchers at Austria's Graz University of Technology. These types of collaborations will proliferate amid digital innovation's multiplicative march.

While cybersecurity sometimes can seem like an arena of digital filled with gloom and doom, in addition to corporate collaborative efforts, there are signs of technological innovation at the intersection of safety. Blockchain is one such innovation.

Blockchain and the Future of Cybersecurity

Blockchain is a high-security approach to many of the cybersecurity issues we've discussed so far.

Its efficacy resides in its ability to split and store sensitive information in multiple locations. It's like cutting up a $20 bill, transforming the pieces into something that doesn't look like currency and placing the pieces in different drawers around your house. It'd be tough for a burglar to find and make use of those pieces. In blockchain, various components of data are recorded by separate parties, making it virtually impossible for someone to steal all of the records that make up a single transaction. Its ability to decentralize record-keeping across a group of willing participants securely is powerfully addressing three central challenges within cybersecurity: preventing cyberattacks, enabling "password-less" authentication and maintaining secure digital identity.

Distributed denial of service (DDoS) attacks are a case in point. Through a DDoS, hackers flood a server holding a critical database with redundant, dummy requests while blocking legitimate requests. Service to those legitimate requests gets denied.

A typical response to DDoS involves segmenting the bad traffic from good traffic and preventing bad traffic from hitting the critical database. At a low level, that's what your email provider is doing when it deletes or routes spam to a dedicated spam folder. Because blockchain segments the data across servers, a DDoS that could impact all of the data is virtually impossible.

As we've already discussed, access via login is one of the most vulnerable points of cybersecurity. What if user and access authentication did not require a login? Blockchain makes this possible by enabling password-less authentication by generating device-specific, secured socket layer certificates. The certificate data is stored securely on the distributed blockchain, and when the device securely links to the blockchain via the mutual certificate, it grants access.

Blockchain is also addressing security concerns with digital identities in unique and powerful ways. Today we carry fragmented digital identities across multiple providers that might include Facebook, a record of financial transactions and/or government documents such as driver's licenses and passports.

To combat fragmentation and to create more secure digital identities, Estonia unified its citizens' digital lives through blockchain. The e-Estonia initiative keeps the digital identity of all its citizens housed on a permissioned blockchain. Estonians can view their personal data through a cryptographically secure digital identity card. Any permissioned third party wishing to view that information must gain approval directly from the individual citizen. Any change to the information is seen and permissioned by all participants. This type of digital, secure and centralized identity gives Estonians access to a host of e-services that includes education, health care, transportation and business support.

E-Estonia shone during the COVID-19 pandemic. While many countries struggled through the shutdown of vital services and schooling, Estonia kept humming right along. The World Economic Forum (WEF) case studied Estonia's response:

"Estonia simply continued to use the thriving, resilient digital infrastructure it had spent decades developing. Digital classrooms, online teaching materials and a huge range of online public services were already in place. Even more crucially, Estonians knew how to access and use them."

Creating a transparent process for going digital and communicating clearly at each stage in the interest of the public trust has catapulted Estonia into a jewel of resilience from which other countries will learn.

Blockchain seems like a cybersecurity slam dunk, but why isn't it more widely adopted? Part of the answer lies in power consumption. Blockchain was born as a technology to facilitate digital currency such as bitcoin. One bitcoin transaction requires more than 5,000 times the energy as using a Visa credit card. Furthermore, constructing a blockchain by adding a new block to the chain involves iterative computation that is often economically prohibitive.

As we move on from cybersecurity, it's important to remember that in digital, it's continually playing catch-up. In all cases, Ben Franklin's maxim "an ounce of prevention is worth a pound of cure" is entirely in play.

2.4 Artificial Intelligence:
The Opportunity of Pandora

Artificial intelligence finds its roots in ancient humanity. The first, self-moving devices that foreshadowed AI launched in the Middle Ages. However, beliefs, dreams, apparitions and curiosity about artificial life take us back nearly three millennia.

Within Hinduism, a faith tradition dating to 2300 B.C.E., Vishnu, a part of the religion's holy, divine trinity, had to establish avatars to ensure that the earth's population could flourish. As you trace this story through centuries and witness the religion's evolution over time, AI seems a natural extension of that narrative.

Adrienne Mayor, a scholar in the Department of Classics in the School of Humanities and Sciences at Stanford University, recently published a book on the topic titled *Gods and Robots: Myths, Machines and Ancient Dreams of Technology*. In it, she says the ancients routinely explored ideas about artificial life and robots.

Mayor links notions of AI to stories contained in ancient Hindu texts such as the *Ramayana* and the *Mahabharata,* the latter of which includes the most famous of the Hindu scriptures, the Bhagavad Gita. She further points to automatons made by the engineer god Vishwakarma and the goddess Maya.

In Greece, the myth of Pandora, introduced in Hesiod's *Theogony,* evidences similar exploration. Mayor argues that in Hesiod's original edition, Pandora was portrayed as an "artificial, evil woman built by Hephaestus and sent to earth on orders of Zeus to punish humans for discovering fire."

"It could be argued that Pandora was a kind of AI agent," Mayor said in an interview about her work. "Her only mission was to infiltrate the human world and release her jar of miseries."

Pandora's box informs how we see and relate to AI, even today. It conjures a smorgasbord of images, metaphors and predictions often grounded in anticipating the unanticipated. To some, AI is frighteningly apocalyptic. To others, AI is merely a functional, subservient and general-purpose technology of our era, equivalent to the steam engine first invented 250 years ago. To still others, it portends the threshold of a fourth industrial revolution that will affect every industry. And to Google's Sundar Pichai, AI is elemental in its power, more profound than electricity and fire for humanity.

No matter its metaphysical or cultural implications, AI is set to drive an economic boost of $14 trillion across 16 industries in 12 economies by 2035. Its impact is thorough and far-reaching, and users are adopting it whether they realize it or not.

Finding a single definition of AI is elusive. The key underlying technologies, what it can and can't do, remain shrouded in mystery. Broadly defined, AI is "a computing system capable of performing functions that generally require human intelligence," and it's categorized into three general levels of evolution:

ANI (artificial narrow intelligence) is capable of a narrow task such as driving or vision.

AGI (artificial general intelligence) is capable of matching general human intelligence across a wide range of areas, such as reasoning or perception.

ASI (artificial super-intelligence) is capable of exceeding human knowledge in all aspects and marking the point of no return for machine supremacy over humans.

For all the hype about "machines taking over" or "humanity at risk," we still sit at the ANI stage. Current ANI technologies include computer vision/ image recognition (identifying objects and images), machine learning (improving software through data), natural language processing (interacting with humans through spoken language) and robotics.

The ANI forms of AI are rapidly integrating into consumers' daily lives, and the tech heavyweights have already integrated AI into their apps, websites and other digital experiences. If you're reading this on an intelligent machine, you already leverage it. Your digital assistant – perhaps Siri, Google Assistant, Alexa or Cortana – uses a form of AI known as natural language processing. When your email provider identifies spam and sorts mail into folders, these activities occur through machine learning. Social networks such as Facebook use computer vision to identify and tag friends in our posts or even to detect suicidal thoughts and send proactive help.

Customer relationship management (CRM) and call centers are also advancing AI, using voice recognition to authenticate a voice and provide online chatbots to automate humanlike interaction. E-commerce providers cross-sell and upsell using recommendations derived from machine learning. Gartner predicts that within the next five years, nearly a quarter of customer interactions will be facilitated by AI and that 75% of retailers will move from pilot to fully operationalized AI customer service.

Even nontechnology firms are accessing AI's power through API, integrating it into their products and experiences. In this way, AI as a service has solidified. IBM's Watson, a deep question-answering computer system that uses natural language processing, is offered as an API for medical diagnoses, providing its intelligence on a subscription basis to doctors and hospitals.

For example, in *WIRED* magazine, Kevin Kelly has said Watson soon could be the world's best diagnostician. He further projected that "the AI on the horizon looks more like Amazon Web Services – cheap, reliable, industrial-grade digital smartness running behind everything, and almost invisible except when it blinks off. This common utility will serve you as much IQ as you want but no more than you need."

As it finds its way into industries, AI is challenging a lot of established and even fundamental beliefs while shifting industry economics and even their competitive landscape. Self-driving cars mean driving without drivers. The existence of robo-advisers implies that investment advice does not need a human investment adviser. Products like Wordsmith suggest that business stories can be written without journalists. That we have retail innovations like Amazon GO implies that shops may not have shopkeepers. Google aptly summarizes the implication:

"In an AI-first world we are rethinking all our products ... and moving from a mobile-first world to an AI-first world."

Consumer trust with AI-enabled devices is already growing. Even with all of the considerations around security, privacy and the specter of a technology oligopoly explored in Big Data: The New Oil, AI's adoption steadily increases.

Victor Hugo once wrote, "On résiste à l'invasion des armées; on ne résiste pas à l'invasion des idées." Often this is paraphrased as, "There is nothing more powerful than an idea whose time has come." So it is with AI. Though we remain at the ANI stage of development, two powerful applications are talked about in connection with AI: the creation of neural networks and, within that innovation, the progress of facial recognition. In dissecting both, a basic framework for tracking AI into the future can form.

Neural Networks & The Human Brain

When we broke down *How the Intelligent Machine Works*, you met 19th century Spanish Nobel laureate Santiago Ramón y Cajal. Google him. He was a neuroscientist, pathologist and histologist specializing in both neuroanatomy and the central nervous system. He was also an artist.

In 2019, the first full-scale exhibition of his work, titled *The Beautiful Brain,* went on exhibit at the University of North Carolina at Chapel Hill's Ackland Museum of Art. He made more than 3,000 drawings centered on the human brain, including neurons and the workings of the inner ear. Their detail and beauty are profound. NPR called them "high tech for the day" and the era's equivalent of an MRI or PET scan.

Cajal, who attended art school, held deep, lifelong artistic aspirations. He once said, "Any man could, if he were so inclined, be the sculptor of his own brain." In doing so, he spoke into being AI and, more specifically, the artificial neural network (ANN), which mimics the physiology and function of the human brain. It is the ANN that enables robots to identify objects, creates photo-realistic fake images of celebrities and even converts thoughts to text.

We've already broken down the components of the brain – how different lobes play a role correlative to an intelligent machine. Our evolutionary difference as humans – what separates us from other species – rests in our forebrain, a densely packed, three-dimensional layer of neurons under the skull. Branches from these neurons form interconnections called synapses, where memory is stored. In perspective, the human brain contains about 100 billion neurons, each connected via synapses to about 10,000 other neurons, cumulatively storing 1 to 1,000 TB of data (1,000 TB is equal to 20 million four-drawer filing cabinets full of text or 500 billion pages of standard printed text).

How does thinking work? When we receive an external stimulus such as vision or sound, data travels as electrical signals through a path between neurons. The specific routes depend on the strength of interneuron connections formed as the result of all previous learning experiences. A neuron may get signals from many other neurons, and if the sum of all input signals crosses its activation threshold, it transmits the signal to the next connection; otherwise the signal dies at that neuron. At its most essential, thinking involves progressing information from one neuron to the next, from input neurons to "thinking" neurons to output neurons. The distance we can travel with raw data is a critical attribute in intelligence. It's why standardized tests such as the SAT, ACT or GRE evaluate our "if, then" or "so what" skillsets.

A facial recognition ANN system follows a similar progression. It involves exposing the system to volumes of photos and a photo identifier (i.e., a name). Once trained, the system takes in information and runs it through multiple layers until it has "thought" it through. Starting with pixels, the initial layers will detect basic features such as a specific color. The next set of layers will abstract them into higher-level features such as a nose. This process will continue until the output layer matches the face with a name. Once the system learns common patterns of a human face (eyes always appear higher than the nose), it speeds up.

To put it in technical terms, the neuron equivalent in ANN is a node. Unlike the three-dimensionally packed neurons, nodes connect to each other in layers – an input layer for getting information, an output layer for generating results and multiple 'hidden layers' in between for processing. Every node assigns a 'weight' to the connection from an incoming node, and its output is the weighted sum of data from each incoming node. If the weighted sum is above the quantitative threshold, the node fires its output to the next connected node. In the active state, each layer of ANN takes information, combines it into the next level of abstraction and passes it to the next layer, until the information reaches the highest level of abstraction at the output layer. The larger the number of layers, the deeper the network is, and hence the phrase "deep learning."

Unlike the brain, ANN randomly assigns the weights and thresholds from the beginning. By running data for known outcomes, the weights and thresholds become optimized, minimizing errors. This "try, try again until you succeed" approach (called supervised learning) extends until it achieves a correct output, at which point ANN is trained.

ANNs are incredibly useful because you don't have to tell them how to do the job. They replace task-specific traditional programming with "learning from data." ANN is working its way into computing, too. As chip manufacturers begin integrating neural engines into the processor, it's only a matter of time before ANN becomes core to our daily lives.

As it advances, Jurgen Schmidhuber, an AI pioneer, has said, "Today's largest [ANN] have a billion connections or so. In 25 years, we should have rather cheap, human-cortex-sized [ANN] with more than 100,000 billion electronic connections. A few decades later, we may have cheap computers with the raw computational power of all of the planet's 10 billion human brains together."

Facial Recognition

We alluded to facial recognition as the prime example of an ANN system. It's both a hot and controversial topic that is poised to impact all of our lives. Often, to grease the skids of change, high-profile events are used to illustrate a technology's novelty while normalizing its power. Take, for example, the 2020 Olympic Games, which were postponed until 2021 because of the COVID-19 pandemic. If they eventually take place, tech giant NEC will showcase its newly developed facial recognition software to identify and authenticate more than 300,000 athletes, volunteers, media personnel and guests.

Meanwhile, Uber's Real-Time ID Check uses driver selfies to verify driver identities before approving passenger rides. And, just three days after installing facial recognition software at leading U.S. airports, U.S. immigration authorities intercepted an imposter posing as a French passport holder at Dulles International Airport in Washington, D.C.

Facial recognition comes naturally to humans (unless you suffer from prosopagnosia – a condition that renders sufferers unable to recognize even their own faces). As we've discussed, facial recognition technology is trained in that same innately human capability using ANN. It comes with differing levels of sophistication and methodologies that include 2D and 3D recognition, skin texture analysis and thermal analysis.

We described 2D facial recognition as we explored the basics of ANN. In 3D facial recognition, the challenges of 2D resolve, including navigating variables such as pose, image quality and lighting quality. It measures and renders a 3D image through the use of various angles or structured light – a known pattern of light. Apple has applied this technology in its Face ID to create 3D digital images of iPhone users' faces, using infrared dots picked up by a camera measured against a stored image to authenticate a user's face. Apple stands by the security of the Face ID feature even in the dark.

Skin texture analysis goes even further. It scans small patches of skin, at the level of fine lines, pores and texture, and translates these into unique mathematical measurements. It makes skin texture facial recognition 20% to 30% more accurate than 3D facial recognition alone. It's even capable of distinguishing between identical twins.

Thermal imaging comes in handy in low light or nighttime conditions. Robust sensors capture a body's thermal infrared waves, converting it into a facial image. DJI, a leading drone manufacturer, uses this approach to power its nighttime search and rescue missions.

While many U.S. cities, states and security agencies are starting their use of facial recognition technology, China has taken it to the next level. The world leader in facial recognition deployment, China is already using an estimated 176 million surveillance cameras and is set to onboard 450 million more. China has fine-tuned facial recognition for "domestic security." In one recent experiment, demonstrating the capabilities of Guiyang's facial recognition system, a BBC reporter was found within the city in just seven minutes.

China expects to implement a national social credit system by the end of 2020 that will calculate a social credit score for each citizen based on multiple data. It will include income tax, utility and credit bills while factoring life markers such as criminal activity, traffic records, shopping habits and social media posts. Once established, the social credit rating will blacklist or approve citizens for travel, insurance, loans, employment, internet access and more.

In China, SenseTime has established itself as the country's "largest and self-developed AI company." While other AI companies use popular open-source operating systems or frameworks, such as Caffe, Torch or TensorFlow, SenseTime has built its own AI platform, Parrots. As of 2018, this platform boasted an astounding 1,207 network layers that could train up to 2 billion facial images simultaneously. According to SenseTime, its facial recognition technology could detect up to 240 vital facial characteristics in a millisecond and could recognize over 10 facial attributes, such as gender, age, expression and facial hair. More amazingly, it could do all this with an error rate of less than 1 in 10,000,000. Most recently, SenseTime claimed to have processed 500 million identities for facial recognition purposes.

Current facial recognition systems are far from perfect, and there are real and valid concerns regarding accuracy, bias and abuse of the technology. Microsoft recently published a strong pitch for public regulation and corporate responsibility for facial recognition. It signals that for AI, it's an evolutionary rite of passage. While accuracy will eventually meet performance expectations, proponents of facial recognition believe that governments will establish protective standards, and millions of end users will benefit from the mainstream adoption of facial recognition technology. Time will tell.

Facial recognition mirrors the whole of AI.

2.5 Augmented and Virtual Reality:
Digital's Alternative Universe

Who knew that the key to augmented reality (AR) "crossing the chasm" to establish a mainstream audience would be through a yellow, cute cartoon monster named Pikachu? Pikachu has long been a central icon for Pokémon (short for Pocket Monsters, the original Japanese name). The character began as a comic in the Japanese gaming magazine *Game Freak*. Even as writer Satoshi Tajiri and illustrator Ken Sugimori debuted their storylines in the 1980s, they also observed that the arcade game scene felt stale. It moved them to develop games under the *Game Freak* banner.

In 1996, Tajiri and Sugimori debuted *Pocket Monsters: Red and Green* on the Nintendo Game Boy. Its franchise blossomed. It moved onto other gaming platforms, created an anime TV show, established a trading card game and became a Comic-Con-meets-E3 blockbuster.

As it evolved, Pokémon evolved into an intricate role-playing and strategy game, but its base premise casts players as fight trainers who scour the globe to catch Pokémons and then teach them to battle each other. The franchise has had a devoted following.

In 2016, the Pokémon Co. – jointly owned by GameFreak and Nintendo – collaborated with game developer Niantic and launched Pokémon GO. Packaged for mobile devices and sold in the App Store for iOS and Google Play for Android, Pokémon GO leveraged GPS and augmented reality, which allowed people to search for Pokémons in their neighborhoods. It means you can hold your phone up in the correct location, and you'll see the camera's image with a Pokémon tooling around on top of it. Players hunt for Pokémons on foot – thus the GO. If you've ever caught Pokémon GO players in action, it's akin to an emergency-meets-modern dance. Perhaps you've seen them running past you on your favorite trail, in a museum or near a café as they wildly attempt to locate and capture a Pokémon they are tracking on their screen.

IGN, the video game website, reported that Pokémon GO surpassed $3 billion in revenue by 2019. Upsells of game add-ons such as the ability to train and trade Pokémons created monetization opportunities. SuperData Research has stated that daily global spend on the game is $2.5 million.

AR and its older sibling, virtual reality (VR), have come a long way, and now that we understand the commercial possibility of this technology, let's define and discover them in detail.

In AR, digital content, like displays, text, sound or video, is added to a device screen, making these additions part of the full physical world picture. In this way, digital content augments reality.

Most smartphones come with AR software in their mobile operating systems. ARKit for Apple devices and ARCore for Android devices enable developers to build AR mobile apps. At their core, as Ars Technica describes, both systems "do a lot of the heavy lifting for app developers in terms of working with the device's camera, scanning images and objects in the environment, and positioning 3D models in real space and making them fit in. They combine device motion tracking, camera scene capture, advanced scene processing, and display conveniences to simplify the task of building an AR experience." Pokémon GO is a perfect example of AR in action.

In contrast, VR refers to a 100% computer-generated view of the world. That view could be a digital rendering of the physical world, fully and creatively imagined, or a combination of reality and imagination put into digital form. To use VR, users cover their eyes with a VR headset such as the Oculus or Vive or smartphone VR accessories such as Google Cardboard or Samsung Gear. In some cases, users don entire bodysuits and gloves. Sensors on these accessories pick user movements to simulate within the immersive and, at this point, almost real time virtual environment.

AR and VR technologies straddle the line between digital and physical worlds, which we'll get into later. This immersive quality is driving vast commercial applicability. TechCrunch believes the installed base of AR could reach 3.5 billion and $90 billion in revenue by 2022, while VR is expected to hit a 50 million installed base and $10+ billion in revenue over that same period.

Growth in both segments is driven by the retail, entertainment, manufacturing and health care industries. In retail, typical AR/VR uses center on helping shoppers answer three questions: How does it look on me? How does it look in my home? How can I find or buy a product? To that end, L'Oréal Paris has developed a virtual makeup try-on experience using Facebook Camera for its leading beauty brands. You take a selfie using Facebook Camera and try makeup, base, mascara and other products.

Swedish ready-to-assemble furniture and all-things-home giant IKEA created an AR app called IKEA Place that enables users to – you guessed it – place 3D models of items in their homes using their mobile devices. Lowe's launched a similar app across its lineup to assist shoppers with design and visualizing projects. Finally, Spanish apparel retailer Zara's AR app increased store traffic among millennials by "showing models wearing selected looks from its ranges when a mobile phone is held up to a sensor within the store or designated shop windows, with customers being able to click through to buy the clothes."

In entertainment, games such as Pokémon GO are the torchbearers of AR adoption. More than 47% of the 13 million installed AR apps on Apple's ARKit are games. MarketWatch expects the AR gaming market to grow at a compounded annual rate of 150%+, reaching $285 billion in revenue by 2023.

Beyond games, AR and VR are being used by leading arts and culture venues around the world to create more immersive and informed content consumption. The French National Museum of History has a dedicated VR room that "highlights the origin of life on earth as well as how human being[s] influence [their] own environment." The Philadelphia Orchestra released its LiveNote AR concert hall app "that allows audiences to access information about the works they are hearing, following the music with realtime musical, emotional, and historical highlights."

In hospitality, Airbnb has created an AR app that enables users to leverage their mobile devices to find things throughout their temporary residence faster and more efficiently.

In manufacturing, implementation of AR and VR has focused on operations and employee training, sparking other opportunities within the sector. In most operational environments, workers access information on screens, papers, binders and boards, and operators must step away from the task at hand and use their hands to find what they need. In an attempt to minimize "manual latency" of these activities, manufacturers are now using AR-enabled smart glasses such as Google Glass and Microsoft HoloLens to deliver real time, hands-free (and potentially voice-controlled) access to information about relevant objects in an operator's field of view. For example, a warehouse worker can use AR to get pertinent, real time information about shipments, including their contents, destination and origin, by merely looking at it through a pair of smart glasses. Forrester Research expects more than 14 million U.S. workers to use smart glasses by 2025.

In terms of employee training, Lockheed Martin started using AR to expedite technician training in the manufacturing of Orion vehicles for NASA with impressive results. *The Wall Street Journal* reported that "before, for example, technicians used paper instructions or 3D models on a computer in certain manufacturing processes of Orion. Now, instead of having to look through binders of data or content on the computer across the room, they can wear an AR device, such as HoloLens, which overlays instructions for drilling or applying torque to specific parts of the spacecraft. ... The time it takes for a technician to 'ramp up,' or to understand the drilling processes has been reduced from eight hours to about 45 minutes using augmented reality headsets."

In health care, AR and VR are used to map patient bodies and offer distractions that mitigate pain while treating patients and aiding physician training. Doctors at Cedars-Sinai Medical Center have used VR headsets with immersive content for pain distraction during procedures for more than 2,500 patients. In burn trauma scenarios, SnowWorld, a VR therapy, helps patients deal with the physical and psychological pain of burn treatment. The Cleveland Clinic leverages a VR-based curriculum to teach clinical anatomy to students, and some hospitals are starting to digitally record rare operations that are used as immersive virtual experiences to train surgeons.

In light of the strength and diversity of these examples and the growth numbers shared above, why isn't AR or VR even more mainstream? An eMarketer survey found that 40% of respondents rated "bulky hardware and technical glitches" as the leading obstacles to the mass adoption of these technologies. Technical resolutions aren't far away. Remember, video moved from tiny clips often marked by buffering issues in the late 1990s on specialized technologies such as RealPlayer to a ubiquitous part of the landscape on any device. The intelligent machine will catch up with speed.

Once it does, several implications emerge for leaders and their businesses. Entertainment will morph into a ubiquitous opportunity. Entertainment at home will focus on gamification and building parallel worlds in which to play. Merchandizing brick and mortar showrooms will receive a deeper layer of entertainment value, too, by offering "endless aisles" and offering production virtualization demonstrations. In human resource and training environments, as we've discussed, learning, maintenance and customer service offerings will get an AR and VR makeover that will offer efficiencies and, after significant upfront investments, save companies significant amounts of money. Finally, throughout the business world, AR and VR will equip companies to reach new markets without any real estate. A new distribution channel for content and engagement will emerge. In industries such as construction, finished buildings can be envisioned, previewed and toured. The travel industry, where authentic virtual visits can fast-track destination desire and decisioning, will undergo a marketing revolution.

Amid this upside arrives a threat. Once AR and VR integrate into the mainstream, they hold power to unseat real-world locations and contexts, up-ending and disrupting several established, deep-seated assumptions around how markets are approached and led and how content is delivered.

2.6 Digital Currency:
Trading Trust for a Puzzle

If big data is the new oil, is digital currency the new gold?

Gold. A rare-earth mineral. First mined in Eastern Europe around 4000 B.C., it served a function in decorative arts. In 1500 B.C., gold became a popular medium for international trade. In the 14th century, Britain shifted its monetary system to what became known as the gold standard. In 1799, a 17-pound golden nugget was found in North Carolina, the first documented discovery in the U.S.; North Carolina supplied all the domestic gold coined at Philadelphia's U.S. Mint through the early 1800s. In 1848, the California Gold Rush started when James Marshall found gold flakes in his pond. In 1900, the Gold Standard Act officially established the U.S. on the gold standard. Later in the century, gold was discovered in South Africa, which now accounts for 40% of all the world's reserves ever mined, and in the Klondike River of Alaska, America's last gold rush began.

Gold was and is a "see and touch investment." It has had a historically lower correlation with stocks and bonds and a low issuer risk, making it especially appealing as a "safe-haven asset" during uncertainties such as inflation and currency depreciation – a characteristic that endures. In the 1970s, the U.S. finally moved away from the gold standard and based currency markets solely on the U.S. dollar.

Digital currency. It offers the ability to authorize transactions digitally and facilitate commerce-related features such as offers, coupons, rewards and electronic receipts. Similarly, brand currency uses a system of reward points and social influence or sharing as the currency. Cryptocurrency, another digital currency variant we'll focus on throughout this chapter, is wholly new. It transcends nations and financial institutions, validating user credentials to facilitate transactions. It's where the gold comparison becomes most relevant and fascinating.

Since their inception in 2009, cryptocurrencies have snowballed to a cumulative market value of $230 billion. Bitcoin, with a market value of $117.81 billion, was the first and continues to be the most popular of all cryptocurrencies. It's incredibly similar to gold. It can be sold or purchased against most currencies and is a recognized medium of exchange. It is tough to steal or hack. Side note of relevance: While gold may seem like a grab and go heist, like in a scene from the movie *The Italian Job*, remember, $1 million in gold weighs roughly 50 pounds and is more than likely stored in the most advanced, high-security vault on the market. Importantly and while all of this is true, bitcoin as the new gold probably comes from two key advantages: its rarity and its independent value.

Bitcoin, like gold, has a limited supply. When you own "x" number of bitcoins, you own some percentage of the total 21 million bitcoins created. All of the other bitcoin generations don't dilute your portion of the aggregate value. What changes your value is something else incredibly similar to gold: the increase in the overall demand for bitcoins against its fixed supply.

The decentralization of bitcoin makes it even more attractive as, in uncertain times, the value of fiat currencies could change as central banks print more money. Bitcoin, like gold, carries an independent value. In a Seeking Alpha post, Matt O'Connor posits an interesting theory: Bitcoin might be severely undervalued compared to gold.

"For example, there are estimated to have been about 6 billion ounces of gold ever mined. At $1,200 an ounce, that means worldwide supplies of gold represent a $7.2 trillion USD value," O'Connor writes. "If we think of those $7.2 trillion roughly as the worldwide demand for non-paper currency, even if we hold it constant and assume Bitcoin is only 1% of this demand, given the current level of about 15.5 million Bitcoins in existence right now, each one would be worth about $4,600 vs. their current price around $400."

Bitcoin and the whole notion that information equals currency quietly began when the bitcoin.org domain name was claimed in August 2008. In October, a white paper circulates among a cryptography mailing list. It is penned by Satoshi Nakamoto and is titled *Bitcoin: A Peer-to-Peer Electronic Cash System*. It detailed how a peer-to-peer network could be used to create a "system for electronic transactions without relying on trust." In January 2009, the bitcoin network launches with Nakamoto "mining the genesis block of bitcoin (block number 0), which had a reward of 50 bitcoins." The line of data encoding it, when put together, read:

The Times 03/Jan/2009 Chancellor on the brink of second bailout of banks

Amid the Great Recession, bitcoin marked its birth by taking a shot at fractional-reserve banking. Its trajectory remains marked by drama, mystery and turbulence. A single bitcoin has been worth as much as $10,000. As of this writing, it hovers in the $9,500 range.

Bitcoin has always been an abstract investment. Its cryptocurrency classification emerged because it originated the blockchain approach to security. You can go to a site like coinbase.com and buy bitcoin against a fiat currency like the U.S. dollar and store it in a secure place. To use it for payment, you then send the bitcoin to another person, just like you do when you wire money to a seller's bank account through PayPal or Venmo. However, to authenticate that transaction, there's a big difference between conventional currency and bitcoin. In a wire transfer, the central bank keeps a record of the transaction (i.e. via a central ledger) for accuracy and future reference.

Through Bitcoin, the ledger system decentralizes through blockchain. In practice, all outstanding bitcoin transactions become grouped into blocks, and each block is linked to a previous block and then recorded by a network of computers using cryptographic technology. In other words, blockchain authenticates transactions via crowdsourcing.

What incentivizes this crowdsourced activity? In return for verification, participants get bitcoin rewards through a process called "mining." Participants may aggregate recent transactions into blocks and try to solve a computationally difficult puzzle. Remember "The Times 03/Jan/2009 Chancellor on the brink of second bailout of banks?"

Blockchain participants – those on whose machines the data is stored – receive an opportunity to solve the puzzle. Whoever solves it first gets to put the next block on the blockchain and also receives newly minted bitcoins as a reward for their hard work. Rewards are not fixed. They undergo diminishing returns and get halved every 210,000th block (spanning roughly four years). At its founding, the reward was 50 bitcoins. That figure reduced to 12 bitcoins by 2017 (just over $52K at today's bitcoin price). If we continue with the math, with 16 million bitcoins in circulation today, the theoretical maximum number of bitcoins in supply is 21 million.

Bitcoin and all cryptocurrencies are luring adoption through a unique blend of gaming, security and meteoric growth. However, an Achilles heel of the entire industry arises in the form of substitution risk. Gold is a unique metal and, despite efforts from metallurgists since the dawn of its value, there is no perfect substitute that carries a similar global mystique. Bitcoin, on the other hand, has already been joined by more than 1,600 cryptocurrency alternatives that are all in use today.

Eric Posner paints an extreme end state impact of bitcoin's easy substitutability in a *Slate* article headlined "Fool's Gold." He writes:

"True, bitcoins cannot be manufactured beyond the limits set by Nakamoto. But there is no way to prevent future Nakamotos from creating bitcoin substitutes – say, bytecoin or botcoin. If merchants are willing to accept bitcoins, they will be willing to accept the substitutes, especially as bitcoins become scarce and consumers scramble for substitutes. If there are no constraints on substitute digital currencies – and there aren't – then the value of bitcoins will plummet as the subs begin to circulate. And once it becomes clear that there is no limit, people will realize that their holdings could become worthless at any moment, and demand for bitcoins and the other currencies will collapse."

As it moves through its second decade, Bitcoin's market cap of $118 billion represents a massive 350-fold increase over the past five years. On the other hand, gold has been tried and tested over 2,000 years, and today there are 287,000 metric tons with an estimated value of over $7 trillion. No doubt that bitcoin is emerging as a complementary "storage of value" to gold, and to date, it's delivered more boom than bust. All of this said, declaring "bitcoin is the new gold"? Definitively premature.

2.7 Sans Display:
The Post-Screen IoT World

No book on digital would be complete without a mention of the 1968 film *2001: A Space Odyssey*. In it, the HAL (Heuristically Programmed ALgorithmic) 9000 computer is a character that interacts with a two-person crew on a mission to Jupiter. In the end, it is HAL, not the crew, who is most in touch with his emotions and seeks to be heard. Near the climax of the story, the crew decides to stop speaking to HAL. This communication breakdown leads HAL to kill one crew member and nearly kill the other.

When filmmakers Stanley Kubrick and Arthur C. Clarke fleshed out their prediction of an AI-driven, digital-voice-activated intelligent machine by 2001, they were just 10 years off the mark. Even though voice recognition began in the 1960s, it wasn't until 2011 that IBM's Watson won the game show *Jeopardy!* and Apple launched Siri, the first mass-market voice assistant.

As previously addressed, digital voice assistants are a form of vocal intelligence (VI) that includes Siri, Amazon Alexa, Google Now and Microsoft Cortana. They showcase the new frontiers of the human-machine interface. Alexa is the brain that enables Amazon Echo to answer commands from "What's the weather today?" to "Switch on the light" to "Order me a pizza."

According to eMarketer, 35 million Americans make use of digital VI at least once a month, and a quarter of all digital searches are voice-activated. When they are, it sets into motion a three-step process of interpretation and response: Speech converts to text, the text translates to intent and intent translates into action.

Speech into text is self-explanatory. VI essentially converts a voice command to the same text input that your computer or smartphone gets from typing. Good speech-to-text software such as Apple Dictation, Google Docs voice typing and Dragon NaturallySpeaking made this viable because they adjust for ambient noise and variation in diction, tone, pitch and accent and are very accurate across languages. *Scienceline* explains how the software works:

"The software breaks your speech down into tiny, recognizable parts called phonemes – there are only 44 of them in the English language. It's the order, combination and context of these phonemes that allows the sophisticated audio analysis software to figure out what exactly you're saying. ... For words that are pronounced the same way, such as eight and ate, the software analyzes the context and syntax of the sentence to figure out the best text match for the word you spoke. In its database, the software then matches the analyzed words with the text that best matches the words you spoke."

The second step, text to intent, interprets exact user meaning. For example, if you say "tell me about Paris" in a conversational context, digital VI quickly attempts to discern your real intent. Are you asking for the latest news about Paris? Flight options to Paris? Current weather in Paris? Paris historic landmarks? Or are you asking about news stories tagged to Paris Hilton? While search engines solve this challenge by ranking answers to the "query" in decreasing order of inferred intent, the bar is significantly higher with digital VI. Vocal intelligence must abstract intent from a conversational input and respond with only one best answer. This fact makes IBM Watson's win over 74-time consecutive champion Ken Jennings so astounding. It did it all through "natural language processing" and tallied the most right "single" answers. Here's how IBM describes this processing within Watson, which the company refers to as DeepQA technology:

"First up, DeepQA works out what the question is asking, then works out some possible answers based on the information it has on hand, creating a thread for each. Every thread uses hundreds of algorithms to study the evidence, looking at factors including what the information says, what type of information it is, its reliability, and how likely it is to be relevant. It then creates an individual weighting based on what Watson has previously learned about how likely they are to be right. It then generates a ranked list of answers, with evidence for each of its options. The information that DeepQA would eventually be able to query for Jeopardy was 200 million pages of information, from a variety of sources."

The final step, intent translated into action, aims to fulfill the user's need. Most digital VIs are evolving from simple questions, such as weather reports, to executing complex operations in increasingly digital devices such as cars, refrigerators, thermostats, lightbulbs and door locks. When intent translates into action, cars move forward, refrigerators cool, houses warm up, lights get turned off and doors lock themselves at night.

These three core capabilities of digital VI – speech to text, text to intent and intent to action – not only get better with more data but are also available as an API from multiple providers. Businesses can leverage that modularity and pick and choose the best options in building an integrated solution for their customers.

Digital VI and the specialized hardware that accompanies it is just one example of the Internet of Things (IoT) – an ever-growing constellation of computing devices, mechanical and digital machines that can communicate and transfer data over a network without human intervention. Through IoT, we'll see how more of the household and specialty devices we use every day are alive, fully connected partners in our lives.

The Internet of Things (IoT)

Let's first step back and revisit IoT nearly two decades ago. In 2006, the IoT was reasonably limited. Most devices already associated with computing were connected, including printers and gaming consoles. Home and enterprise networks emerged and leveraged connectivity to control thermostats, run security cameras and power and modulate refrigerators. Streaming consoles began migrating entertainment and other forms of video, film and audio from the internet to previously disconnected television sets. Fitness trackers emerged that monitored the body and its movements to track progress and gauge performance.

Today, there are more than 8.4 billion connected things, and here's just a sampling of what that includes:

Watches
Clothing/jewelry
Sleep trackers
Glasses
UV monitors
Health monitors
Televisions
Cameras
Sporting goods

Lightbulbs

Switches and receptacles

Water heaters

Smoke detectors

Locks

Blinds

Garage doors

Ovens/slow cookers

Automobiles

Drones

Coffeepots

Parking meters

Globally, there is an appetite for more connection and more expectation of connection. That's in direct proportion to more internet accessibility. As more people gain opportunities to connect digitally and more companies begin producing goods that leverage that access, more people start using and living more of their lives on the internet. In 2010, there were 2 billion people around the world using the internet for two hours a day. In 2019, 4.39 billion used the internet for more than six hours a day. As you can imagine, these numbers continue ticking upward day by day.

This increase also has speed to thank as a driver. In 2005, 2G cellular service, DSL modems and 802.11g wireless routers were offering internet access at basically the same rate and well under 250 Mbps (megabytes per second). It was adequate for email, low graphics, low-resolution video, web browsing, and talking and texting.

In 2010, WiFi took off, and the latest 802.11n protocol was able to hustle above 500 Mbps. Wired connections through cable modems facilitated nearly 250 Mbps. Cellular went through its renaissance, moving from 2G to 3G to 4G, and could almost surpass the 150 Mbps.

By 2015, speed gained steam. Wireless 802.11ac technologies and a fully wired infrastructure through fiber optics boosted velocity to 1 Gbps. Cellular was still lagging and yet showing promise with the rollout of 4G LTE ADV connectivity that finally surpassed 250 Mbps and could facilitate gaming and videoconferencing.

Since 2015, speed has "hockey sticked." Wireless 802.11x and cellular 5G connectivity have left wired connectivity in the dust and are enabling speeds surpassing 10 Gbps and set to close on 20 Gbps. Acceleration of this magnitude is disruptive – particularly when it comes to 5G, as it will be the most accessible and easiest to install technology across the globe.

Like no other digital topic, IoT, when looked at in concert with AI, AR and VR, exemplifies the convergence of the digital and physical worlds. This notion drives what's next in our journey: a climb in altitude that will give us a high-level view of digital. From that place, the walls break down, and we investigate how digital is fully collaborating in physical environments across industries.

Part 3
Phygital: Where Worlds Converge

Phygital. It means the bridging of the physical and digital worlds. It's a concept that often evokes the natural combination of both. In this last part of our journey, we'll see this notion is changing. Tectonic plates within both the physical and digital realms are shifting and creating quakes across the whole of business.

Forrester Research has predicted that as we march toward 2025, "we will fully be in a transition period between separated and tightly blended physical and digital experiences in our work and lives."

Throughout Part 3 of this book, we'll examine why and how the notion of phygital is on a relentless, jaw-dropping march. We back out to the 30,000-foot level and peer across industries to understand the tide of digital and where it might head next. To prepare us to do so, let's note how the five building blocks inside an intelligent machine are fostering these sweeping strategic shifts in the way industries leverage convergence.

In *storage*, extended and persistent memory enables learning and remembering more about customer preferences, personalization and plans. *Computing's* decreasing costs and increasing power, particularly in mobile hardware, provide the potential for meaningfully convergent digital solutions. *Software* delivers on the possibility of that hardware by offering value through useful and easy-to-use customer experiences.

Connection is everywhere, and in particular, the growing ubiquity of a wireless internet combined with device-to-installation connectedness provides both global and local communications and awareness. *Sensor* diversity and complexity flourish as radios, beacons, NFC, GPS, cameras and biometric scanners allow for more contextually relevant experiences.

We are not only ripe for convergence – we *are* converging. Some industries and companies are doing so with more fluidity than others, and, while the specific use cases are a function of the organizational context, the industry, the competition and the supporting ecosystem, three evolutionary steps typically characterize digital innovation: 1) market and sell existing products, 2) enhance the value of the core customer experience and 3) offer completely new products that are simply not possible without digital. Let's examine each of these in turn.

In most organizations, digital innovation manifests itself (and funds itself) through digital marketing and e-commerce because both of these open the enterprise to new markets and digital epiphanies. Importantly, it's an easy sell, as e-commerce is a world of untapped opportunity. Most organizations can build direct e-commerce capabilities on the web, iOS and Android platforms, and, additionally, many industry verticals leverage Amazon, eBay, and Alibaba – massive digital marketplaces that aggregate consumer demand. With e-commerce amounting to less than 10% of U.S. retail sales, there's still significant headroom for growth. As Hans Tung wrote in TechCrunch:

"Vast swaths of e-commerce dollars remain to be created and claimed. Projecting forward, the e-commerce market segmentation may end up looking more like traditional retail but with a new twist on shopping as an experience, and likely aided by AR/VR technology and artificial intelligence. ... Successful e-brands and vertical marketplaces such as Airbnb, Xiaohongshu, Pinterest and Houzz are expert at creating a social following, creating both inspirational and aspirational sense of community. Personalization of products and cultivation of community then drive users to project these brands outwards on social media."

Leveraging digital to enhance the end-to-end customer experience is a next-step transformation that reaps almost immediate dividends for brand loyalty and sales. Examples of this include call centers using integrated voice and chat applications for improving agent productivity and customer satisfaction; retailers enhancing in-store experiences for shoppers through digital showrooming; and industrial railroads improving efficiency and customer safety through sensor-enabled predictable maintenance. This type of innovation needs a good understanding of the existing product capabilities and customer needs, even as it leverages mainstream digital capabilities to create a seamless experience for the customers. Craig Borowski gives an excellent overview of seamless customer experience in his *Harvard Business Review* post titled, "What a Great Digital Customer Experience Actually Looks Like":

"Many companies clumsily add digital components to customer journeys that don't directly benefit the customer or are superfluous to the company's value proposition. At best, these additions fail to gain traction; at worst, they can make the experience more complicated or confusing and drive people away. For months now, a regional deli I frequent has been asking me to answer an online survey. With every meal I purchase, the cashier highlights on the receipt the web address they'd like me to visit to complete the survey. But my customer journey with this sandwich shop never had any digital components. Why would they expect me to go online and complete their survey now? 'Digital' and 'online' are not synonyms for convenient. ... A better approach is to design an app that simplifies some aspects of the journey on which customers are already engaging. Save them time and effort; don't ask for more of either. The Starbucks mobile app is a great example of this. It manages a customer's loyalty points and lets customers place orders ahead of time, so they can skip the in-store lines. Customers love that the app saves them time."

The last evolutionary step in initiating digital transformation rests in businesses' building completely new, digitally enabled products that otherwise would not be possible without the scale, speed and distribution economics of digital. While this context typically plays to the advantage of startups, it's not uncommon to have organically nondigital organizations make an aggressive play. The most well-known and successful example of this type of innovation is Netflix. It made a rapid transition first from DVD distribution to digital streaming and then made a huge leap to original content. In 2020, Netflix's programming grabbed more Emmy nominations than any other producer of original content. Julie Bort detailed this process in a *Business Insider* article, quoting then-Netflix Chief Product Officer Neil Hunt:

"We knew streaming, the internet, was the disruption. Very few businesses get to survive disruption. Usually, the incumbent dies, and the challenger succeeds. We didn't want to be the incumbent," Hunt said. "Streaming video required a much bigger investment in technology than mailing DVDs.

"By combining a data-driven focus and streaming video, Netflix was able to respond to another potential threat: the possibility that networks would stop letting it stream their shows. So, the company was able to transform itself once again into an original studio."

While the three steps we've discussed vary in complexity, know this: They are happening. In nearly every company, in almost every industry, in virtually every country around the world. We'll look at a few. We'll begin by discussing the convergence point itself and how the destiny of reality between physical and digital worlds is playing out philosophically and practically. We'll then take dives into five sectors: health care and pharmaceutical, financial services, automobile, government and retail. We'll end by looking at how phygital is transforming careers and human capital in total by looking at how AI and automation are bending toward the white-collar workforce. Along the way, you will receive the tools you need to ascertain how phygital impacts your industry and how to anticipate where it will go next.

3.1 Convergence:
Shifting Reality

Some believe that convergence of physical and digital realities is a natural extension of what's next. It holds transformative possibilities in our lives. It can solve pressing, real-world problems. It can make a lot of people a lot of money. In this way, it offers a blend of the Apollo 11 lunar landing, Henry Ford's Model T and the first artificial heart transplant: Game-changing technology meets industry and the heart-warming power to extend human life. Within this decadent optimism exists a shadow side, of which you should be aware.

Sam Lessin, a former VP for product at Facebook, is also the co-founder of Fin, a venture focused on "unlock[ing] the missing data your organization needs to connect the dots between process and outcomes and drive continuous improvement of people, process, and tools." I raise his credentials because he is a native digital operator who is on the front lines of phygital. Writing in *The Information*, a Bay Area-based digital publication focused on tech, Lessin lays out a grim counterpoint to the sometimes-endless corporate optimism around digital's role. He raises this question:

"Is the destiny of the internet to become an integrated extension of the physical world, a separate parallel universe, or to supplant and subsume the real world of today?"

He then portrays how the physical world, an open, global and one-time ally of the internet, has turned on it. He posits that the material world is "attacking the open and free space of the internet." He points to newly formed digital borders, regional elimination of specific apps and the move to control speech online. He also says the "internet and meme-driven culture and power structures are starting to actively attack physical institutions as well." He then discusses how internet-fueled movements and power structures have directly translated to political protests in cities across the United States. Lessin believes COVID-19 has intensified the conflict by escalating the importance of digital in day to day life.

Lessin lays out a six-part argument for how and why these competing power structures are at war. In either reality he cautions that no matter if you agree with him at a moral or political level, there are two things to watch as convergence unfolds:

"First, we are watching these abstract conflicts and beliefs come into practical focus as the internet and the physical world go to war. Neither side is going to give up without an explicit fight. Second, even if you believe in internet culture and meme-driven power, when it spills over into the physical world and attacks physical institutions, it is unclear how to deescalate that conflict. Reality still matters. So long as the world is not actually abundant, and we live with the realities of scarce resources and zero-sum allocations, hierarchical power structures and organizations are critical to our existence. So be careful when you attack them."

I've dropped Lessin's commentary into this book because even as we dip our toes into how phygital plays out in industry, you should be aware of its broader philosophical context. This is how some people on the leading edge of organic digital are thinking. Often we feel like tech is removed from us – out there and in our control, except for sudden, addictive scrolls of our Twitter feeds. It's not unlike picking up *The New York Times* a couple of years ago and reading about how many Silicon Valley technology execs – Steve Jobs was one of them – curbed or eliminated their kids' technology use. Digital is powerful stuff. It's not to be handled lightly and requires thoughtfulness and clear-eyed depth.

Lessin is reminiscent of the 20th century's Marshall McCluhan. McCluhan was the midcentury communication theorist and academician who foretold the internet. He is most famous for the quote, "The medium is the message," meaning the physical nature of a given technology not only holds utility – it also says something. Its form and function carry meaning.

Balancing these sobering vantage points, remember that, to date, matter still matters, and the integration of the physical and digital is in its nascent stages. Proclamations that seem crystalline today ultimately may be proven plain wrong.

For example, in 2015, TechCrunch declared that "Uber, the world's largest taxi company, owns no vehicles. Facebook, the world's most popular media owner, creates no content. Alibaba, the most valuable retailer, has no inventory. And Airbnb, the world's largest accommodation provider, owns no real estate." The message was clear: These companies were the "thin interface on top of supply systems." They had eliminated the physical side of their businesses because being the online interface was where the money was.

TechCrunch evoked a giddiness once reserved for an eternal dot-com boom, and it was equally flawed. Many digital leaders, across multiple industries, have rapidly expanded into the physical space. TechCrunch had to walk back these statements three years later and, to illustrate its point, it good-naturedly wrote, "The world's largest taxi firm, Uber, is buying cars. The world's most popular media company, Facebook, now commissions content. The world's most valuable retailer is now Amazon, and it has more than 350 stores. And the world's largest hospitality provider, Airbnb, increasingly owns real estate."

We often think about how brick and mortar is in jeopardy, particularly within the retail space. Store closures and bankruptcies among the likes of Toys R Us, RadioShack and others that reinforce as much. However, there are poignant examples of some retailers bucking this trend– take Best Buy, Sephora, Starbucks or The Home Depot. However, brick-and-mortar is not dying. It's retooling and reimagining the entire experience.

This way of reframing convergence is at once necessary and useful because it forces us to balance the digital and physical realms. As you likely know, leading digital firms such as Google, Facebook, Amazon and Tencent enjoy increasing returns as they scale via network effects. They not only grow fast by creating significant value for users, but they capture a disproportionate share of the rewards, with a minimal physical presence. This fact raises an important question: In such a lucrative digital economy, why do digital players need physical spaces and products?

The answers emerge through three of the most common drivers responsible for "online going offline." First, technological know-how exists to leverage it. Second, upgraded user expectations demand it. Finally, distribution challenges within industry structures are forcing it.

In terms of technological capacity, look no further than Amazon Go, Amazon's chain of nearly 30 convenience stores operating in Chicago, New York, San Francisco and Seattle. Go represents Amazon's master blend of critical technological bits of intelligence gleaned from its digital platforms that are integrated into the store, transforming the physical retail experience.

Amazon has differentiated Go as a Just Walk Out Shopping retail experience. Customers enter the store, browse and leave with what they want. Through a network of ceiling cameras, this "Go" capability, based on computer vision technology, tracks whether an item moves off the shelf. It eliminates the need for the multistep, traditional process of getting in line, scanning products and paying before departure. Instead, the Amazon Go app bills patrons for items they carry out of the store. Conversely, if the customer puts the item back on the shelf, the technology removes it from his or her virtual basket.

Lyft's collaboration with the auto industry offers another example wherein the technology is ready to transform a physical experience. As a key leader in self-driving technology, Lyft is partnering with auto manufacturers to expand its autonomous vehicle technology that will eventually lead to a self-driving Lyft vehicle. It's a technology commercialization exchange that offers a win-win. Lyft reaps the benefits of its autonomous vehicle network while bringing digital technology into the day-to-day life of consumers. Auto manufacturers also gain access to invaluable driving data for research and development through Lyft's network of self-driving vehicles.

Now let's turn our attention to how user expectations drive digital-to-physical migration. Retailers are finding that consumers want it all. This fact has driven successful e-commerce-exclusive firms from "online only" to hybrid online and brick-and-mortar models.

Ilyse Liffreing reported on this trend on the digital-meets-culture site Digiday. She showcased brands such as sustainable shoemaker Allbirds, optical designers Warby Parker and vintage-inspired indie fashion and luxury bedding retailer ModCloth. These companies have all counterintuitively augmented online-exclusive storefronts with brick and mortar locations because, as Liffreing states, "regardless of how convenient online shopping is, consumers still like to visualize, try-on and feel products before purchasing them."

Boll & Branch co-founder and CEO Scott Tannen put this way: "The main reason a customer wouldn't buy our product online was because they wanted to be able to feel it themselves," he said. "We are remedying that with our physical location."

Finally, some digital firms have no choice but to go physical because of distribution challenges in the existing industry structure. Amazon's purchase of Whole Foods is a (no pun intended) prime example, even though the marriage of e-commerce and groceries has always been a tricky proposition. In the late 1990s, a host of online grocery retailers such as Peapod and Webvan emerged with the promise of quick delivery and fresher products that underwent fewer touches from farm to table.

Webvan was a famous fail within the grocery space. A big reason for that? It felt it necessary to create a stand-alone, industry-bypassing distribution model from scratch, building never-before-tried algorithmic software to run fully automated warehouses. It signed Bechtel, the global construction and engineering firm, to a $1 billion contract for designing and building these distribution hubs in several regions throughout the country valued at $30 million each. There was just one problem: They didn't work. It is an icon of the dot-com bust, going from $800 million in initial financing to zero in only three years.

It's this type of failure that drove Amazon to seek out a last-mile distribution hub for grocery and other merchandise. When it bought the upscale, organic grocer Whole Foods Market, *The Atlantic* projected that "Whole Foods' urban and suburban locations are so valuable for

Amazon's delivery business that the deal could be worth it even if the grocer all but stopped selling food. Amazon did not just buy Whole Foods grocery stores. It bought 431 upper-income, prime-location distribution nodes for everything it does." Time will test this opinion.

Sometimes the distribution challenge isn't because of an established supply chain. Sometimes it's due to fierce competition. Spotify, the leading online music-streaming service, appears to be testing a branded Bluetooth home speaker dubbed Home Thing. It began doing so because Apple was reportedly not keen on integrating its Spotify Connect feature into Apple's HomePod and Apple Watch. In this case, it was last-foot distribution that fueled Spotify's move.

While the three drivers we've just explored offer evidence of convergence amid complex drivers, they also provide a gateway to understanding what it will take to be successful in the age of convergence. Digitally wise companies will focus on critical ways to leverage wholly new phygital possibilities across their industries. They will take advantage of mobile's technological ubiquity. They will find ways to leverage digital to streamline end-to-end experiences and product fulfillment. Importantly, they will also seriously evaluate their customer, asking, "Are there ways digital can enhance the total customer experience? Can we gain relevance with customers by offering persistent access and convenience and creating meaningful two-way connections with those customers?"

As we prepare to explore convergence industry-by-industry, one thing is clear: Hoping that digital is a passing fancy is no longer an option. Even though the hotel industry reportedly funded high-level espionage and sting operations at Airbnb and taxi operators protested and fought legal battles with Uber, both have been powerless to stop the phygital wave. Better to transform.

3.2 Health Care and Pharma:
Frictionless Care and Greater Transparency

Remember HIPAA? It's the Health Insurance Portability and Accountability Act. It created the first privacy standards for patient records. It was a forerunner to digital medical records that required new levels of security. It also paved the way for ever-increasing biometric and telemedicine advances that are beginning to turn the tide in patient empowerment tied to personal health.

Also, remember how pharmaceutical companies used to be the sole owners of efficacy data tied to the impact of their products? In other words, they were the gatekeepers around whether their drugs or vaccines worked. Digital has changed that by offering new resources to patients for discussing, reviewing and dialing in treatments for specific conditions while understanding side effects and efficacy timelines.

Hopefully, jogging your memory on both fronts evokes tiny examples from the last 20 years and illustrates how health care and pharma are undergoing a full-scale transformation that offers fertile ground for digital-physical convergence. A significant factor is cost containment.

Costs were one of three driving forces behind drugstore retailer CVS's 2018 acquisition of insurance giant Aetna for nearly $70 billion. Through its purchase, CVS sought to "make health care local and accessible [and to] simplify how consumers access care and lower costs."

Digital will play a significant role. CVS Health Chief Digital Officer Firdaus Bhathena has said, "CVS Health wants to connect the physical and digital experience to expand consumers' access to care," adding that Netflix set the tone for ease of payment and access.

More disruptive moves have followed. Amazon, Berkshire Hathaway and JPMorgan Chase have joined forces to develop Haven, a nonprofit health care firm. It started as a direct attempt to form an independent health care company for their employees to cut costs. As it solidified its corporate trajectory, Haven reassured the industry that it doesn't seek to uproot the existing system but to improve it. Its former CEO, Dr. Atul Gawande, has said Haven seeks to be "an advocate for the patient and an ally to anyone – clinicians, industry leaders, innovators, policymakers, and others – who makes patient care and costs better."

Haven has spent its first two years gearing up. Amazon acquired PillPack, an online pharmacy, and rolled out a telehealth capability for employees while supporting data storage through Amazon Web Services for hospitals and health systems. Time will tell whether this tech-first health insurer can succeed.

Even so, *The New York Times* reported that its launch "landed like a thunderclap – sending stocks for insurers and other major health companies tumbling. Shares of UnitedHealth Group and Anthem plunged."

Let's unpack what both CVS and Haven mean in an industry representing 18% of U.S. GDP. While both moves stand to transform the face of health care, they are more likely not ushering in a digital wave; instead, they're driven by it. Both companies went digital because it reduces friction throughout the end-to-end patient experience. It has upgraded the personalization of preventive and diagnostic care and direct patient connections. It has removed financial barriers in drug discovery and development.

If you've been to a doctor, you don't need a primer on the patient experience. The most inconvenient part of seeing a doctor is often actually going to see the doctor and experiencing the hassles that surround the appointment. According to a survey by Accolade, patients' top concerns in health care include coordinating different aspects of benefits and health care (55%), selecting and understanding benefits (50%) and managing care across different doctors, specialists and facilities (41%).

Digital innovators have taken note and are building products to transform end-to-end patient experiences. They've started simply, focusing first on the basics – such as scheduling a doctor appointment.

According to a Merritt Hawkins study of physicians' offices, the average wait time for patients to have an appointment with a new doctor is 24 days. In larger cities, the average can be as long as 32 days. A new scheduling app, Zocdoc, addresses this issue head-on, helping patients find nearby doctors in their network, browse reviews by other patients and book appointments all within a single app. Zocdoc seeks to facilitate appointments within three days for its 6 million monthly patients, but, because of this relatively straightforward digital technology, the vast majority get appointments within 24 hours.

In 2017, Accenture predicted that by the early 2020s, 64% of patients would schedule appointments digitally and the top 100 U.S. health systems would provide digital self-scheduling capabilities. As of this writing, nearly half of patients schedule online, and almost 80% say they prefer digital scheduling.

Another arena of dramatic change has emerged through telehealth services wherein patients visit doctors remotely, online. Amid the global, 2020 COVID-19 pandemic, this emerged as a significant driver of emergency digital transformation as health care providers of all types attempted to remain viable and technology firms sought to cash in on that need. Key innovators in the space include MDLIVE and Teladoc, both of which offer a 24/7/365 video/phone base consultation platform that costs a subscribing health care practice less than $40 per appointment. They have a 10- to 15-minute average response/callback time and offer an easy way to write and fulfill digital prescriptions.

In addition to the improvements in end-to-end patient experience, these innovations are enabling care for patients in remote geographic locations and giving patients of diverse socioeconomic levels greater access to care.

Importantly, when it comes to personalizing preventive and diagnostic care, digital is disintermediating traditional supply chains and access points, enabling health care systems and new Medtech health care ventures to serve patients directly. It's proven most effective when focused on the chronic conditions responsible for a majority of health care costs such as diabetes, mental health and cardiac issues. Virta is a Medtech firm that boasts actual reversals in type 2 diabetes for patients who use the site's individualized treatment plans. Its objective is to reverse the disease in 100 million sufferers by 2025. Registered Virta patients enter data on their blood pressure and glucose levels through smartphone apps and get personalized interventions on nutrition and other behaviors through education, support from health coaches and peers and medication management by physicians.

For parents of young children, Kinsa, using digital technologies, leverages smart thermometers in its emphasis on earlier detection and response to stop the spread of contagious illness. It takes accurate fever readings and, using analytics around those readings, offers guidance through its mobile app on symptoms, diagnoses and medication doses. During COVID-19, the NBA leveraged it to keep players in the "bubble" tracked and safe during the 2020 mini-season that took place at a single venue in Orlando, Fla.

CardioSecur, a firm focused on cardiac health, "turns your smartphone into a mobile, personalized ECG in just three steps" by attaching a cable to a smartphone, capturing ECG data in 10 seconds and receiving actionable feedback, including, if necessary, a message to "See your cardiologist NOW." All of these offerings enhance accurate health data from wearable technologies such as smartwatches as well as leveraging direct-to-consumer genetic testing kits from third parties such as Ancestry.com.

Pharma also feels the power of digital. Digital significantly impacts drug discovery and development, the leading barriers in bringing drugs through the FDA approval process and to market. In 2016, the average total cost of getting a new drug from invention to the pharmacy was about $2.9 billion. In 2020, *JAMA* reported that the average cost was $1.3 billion. Some of the credit for that decrease goes to digital.

At the drug discovery stage, quantum computing can facilitate molecular simulations that replace the traditional trial-and-error approach of experiments on biological specimens, making the drug discovery process four times faster at a quarter of the cost. At the drug development stage, more than 90% of drugs entering clinical trials fail mainly due to the difficulties in recruiting trial patients and logistical challenges of collecting patient data. Innovations such as the digital trials platform Clinpal and clinical trial portals such as Pfizer Link and Science 37 mean that a combination of web/app interfaces and social media can be used to recruit a more extensive and more diverse sample of trial patients. Scientists also receive accurate health data in real time.

COVID-19 has provided a telling case study in the advancement of digital within pharma by accelerating and expanding vaccine trials to address the virus. Esteemed British medical journal *The Lancet* has created a digital dashboard dubbed the COVID-19 Clinical Trial

Registry that "collates all trials" to "avoid unnecessary duplication of efforts" worldwide. It pulls data from the International Clinical Trials Registry Platform. It includes the Chinese Clinical Trial Registry; ClinicalTrials.gov; the Clinical Research Information Service, Republic of Korea; the EU Clinical Trials Register; ISRCTN; the Iranian Registry of Clinical Trials; the Japan Primary Registries Network; and the German Clinical Trials Register.

The Lancet has also created an AI-originated search methodology to "identify potential clinical studies not captured in trial registries. These methods provide estimates of the likelihood of importance of a study being included in our database, such that the study can then be reviewed manually for inclusion." Doing so saves *The Lancet* 50%-80% of the time "required to manually review all entries without loss of accuracy."

To end this section, let's go back to where this all started: HIPAA. Historically, the profit pool in the hospital-payer-provider ecosystem has been captured primarily by pharma. In the future, this profit model might shift because the key to most of the health care innovations we discussed – particularly personalized preventive care and improved drug discovery and development – is powered by patient data. As you now know, Big Data is the new oil. As the majority of patient data sits with providers, it's not inconceivable that it will capture the majority of the upside from digital transformation. If and when that happens, it may prove to be the most substantial disruption we've seen in health care to date.

3.3 Financial Services:
Money Transformed

Fintech is the newest buzzword in the financial services industry. Fintech is a mashup of the words *financial* and *technology*, but its impact is reaching every segment of the financial services market. It encompasses all the digital technologies used to deliver financial services. Its growth has proven aggressive – from $6 billion in all of 2013 to $6.1 billion in just the first quarter of 2020. Along the way, it is disrupting nearly everything in its path. As we've touched on at other points, fintech has received a lot of help that has powered its adoption and market opportunity.

Within fintech, we'll touch on a few segments undergoing significant transformation due to digital: retail banking, payments and wealth management. Through each, we'll track traditional financial institutional practice and then veer into China, where fintech is dominant and pioneering.

In retail banking, perhaps you remember ING. ING was a Dutch bank with a bright orange brand identity and a nifty marketing approach. In 2000, it was the first to offer American consumers exclusively online checking and savings accounts. Later, it opened brick and mortar cafes that offered ATMs and great coffee. In 2012 it was acquired by Capital One, which maintained the cafes and expanded sales efforts in-store.

ING created a niche driven by one significant understanding: More than 60% of costs for a retail bank come from branches and associated staff. However, ING did more than reduce overhead, and its impact was twofold. First, it made the banking establishment hustle to focus on transaction automation through online accounts, online account transfers, automated alerts, virtual bill payments and mobile check deposit. But it also opened the floodgates for more online banks.

Online banks have no traditional brick and mortar branches. Instead, they pass some of the savings from branch and staff costs to customers in the form of higher savings rates. In the U.S, online banks generally offer a 1% interest rate on a savings account – that's roughly 20 times more than at a retail bank. They are also more efficient in targeting and signing up new customers. Ally Bank, formerly the auto loan wing of GM known as GMAC, is a U.S.-based institution that offers checking and savings accounts, auto loans, mortgages and auto financing. It's the 18th-largest bank in the U.S., with more than 6 million customers. Banks like Ally use a proprietary KYC technology to open accounts online. With some banks, you can access your account within just eight minutes!

Banking also feels the impact of lending's digital shift. Loans from traditional institutions require personal or commercial financial history and documentation. It might include forwarding tax returns, financial or salary statements and appraiser or inspector reports. Assuming error-free documentation, lenders then secure and analyze credit score worthiness. Approval takes time. In the digital world, many of these steps can be automated, expedited or even eliminated. Here, fintech firms are seizing the day. A variety of digital tools such as 24/7 virtual loan centers, cloud document uploads, automated income and asset verification, real time credit score acquisition, e-signatures and chatbots accelerate transactions and make for fluid user experiences. A lending process that used to take a week or more can now be completed within one to three days, even as it provides more flexibility on the total amount financed and maturity.

Kabbage, a commercial lender to small businesses, lends on the basis of an algorithm. Kabbage prospects input personal and business-related information. Then they connect all of their online bank, social media (Facebook) and fintech accounts (PayPal or QuickBooks). Kabbage bases creditworthiness on a combination of weighted factors based on what they see going on within each account. Big Data analytics then handles the whole of the loan underwriting process, and financing is automated.

Payment technology was arguably the very first financial service to be disrupted by digital. In the 1990s, Paytrust became the first digital bill payment service. PayPal, another first-generation web pioneer, built trust among consumers to the point that they agreed to connect their bank accounts and began handling multiple purchases across the internet and beyond. Concurrently, PayPal established a network of B2B relationships with retailers and eventually became a plug and play app that has evolved into a ubiquitous way to transfer money between parties.

Payment innovations have continued their disruptive advance. Alipay and WePay offer examples of online payment innovators. Apple Pay and Samsung Pay use near field communication (NFC) to facilitate digital payments without a credit or debit card at checkout lines and other point of sale destinations such as gas pumps or vending machines. Venmo and others like it are shaking up peer-to-peer (P2P) money transfers via mobile apps.

In China, *The New York Times* has reported on the rise of digital payments and how they are rendering cash obsolete. The country is systematically phasing out cash. Alipay and WeChat pay are the leading options presented by restaurant servers in major cities, with "cash as a third, remote possibility." Facing regulatory concerns on the consumer side that are stifling growth in China's $7 trillion payments market, Ant, Alipay's parent company, and Tencent, WeChat pay's parent, have gone global. Both are surpassing traditional credit card brands such as Visa and MasterCard in total global transactions per day. Even more staggering is Ant's pre-IPO valuation that bankers have set at $200 billion. Even before going public, Ant nearly equals MasterCard's $293 market cap.

This talk of investment brings us to digital at the intersection of wealth management. It's an industry that stewards $220 trillion worldwide. Despite innovators such as Charles Schwab (no commissions!), wealth managers serving high net worth clients typically charge fees equivalent to 1%-3% of assets under management (AUM). In bull markets, clients of advisers are charged more money despite no change in service levels. In the era of digital, customers resent the model and are seeking a different way to do business. Robo-advisers are doing just that, with algorithms providing financial advice to customers with little or no human intervention. It's automating every aspect of wealth management, including risk-adjusted asset allocation, investment selection, order execution, portfolio rebalancing, reporting and tax management. A robo-adviser is available at any hour, can perform high-speed transactions and can be accessed with no account minimum. The AUM fee can be as low as 0.25%. Robo-based providers vary from fintech upstarts Personal and Betterment to established wealth managers such as Charles Schwab and Vanguard.

For all of these advances that are impacting the corners of the traditionally slow-moving financial services sector, another side effect of fintech may prove to be the most significant: how it's helping individuals who have been underserved by traditional financial institutions. As we explore next, China is leading this charge and developing one of the most vibrant fintech ecosystems today.

China, Fintech and Warp Speed

Retail banking and lending are core economic activities for any functioning economy and enjoy attractive profitability. At last count, China had more than 4,500 financial institutions supporting a GDP of $14.3 trillion. Yet only 25% of the 900 million individuals covered by the People's Bank of China (PBOC) credit reference center have access to a credit card.

Why would traditional financial institutions still underserve customers in the areas of banking and lending? It's a phenomenon driven by three factors: high customer acquisition and operating costs, an inability to match digital service level expectations from customers, and insufficient credit histories for some consumers. Fintech firms are structurally advantaged in each of these areas.

As we've learned, to acquire and serve new customers, traditional banks have to invest in physical branches, IT infrastructure and staff labor. In China, this costs a traditional bank nearly $45 per customer. Chinese fintech firms such as WeChat Pay and Ant Financial have unique access to 900 million highly engaged digital customers. Tencent, the world's largest video game company and WeChat owner, spun out WeChat Pay. Alibaba, the Chinese equivalent of Amazon, owns a 33% share in Ant. For both companies, customer acquisition is just a click away, making the acquisition cost close to marginal. Both fintech firms have simpler, more streamlined product portfolios supported by a distributed cloud IT architecture. It results in an average IT operating cost of less than $1.50 per account. Traditional Chinese banks operate at nearly $15 an account, and traditional U.S. banks? Nearly $100 per account. These nontrivial differences in customer acquisition and account operating economics give fintech firms a significant cost-to-serve edge, and many are already exclusively leveraging digital channels to find and onboard new customers.

Going forward, more and more fintech firms will use digital channels exclusively for lowering their cost of customer acquisition. PricewaterhouseCoopers believes "social media will be the primary medium to connect, engage, inform and understand customers ... as well as the place where customers research and compare banks' offerings."

Throughout this book, we've discussed how customer expectations are a major influencer in shaping digital strategy. In China, these expectations are meeting warp speed with another Tencent affiliated institution, WeBank. At WeBank, the average loan approval time is 0.3 seconds, and its technology infrastructure can handle up to 240,000 transactions per second. Over the last three years, it has rolled out 24/7 customer service and an advanced chatbot functionality to reduce its labor cost for outbound security and verification calls by 75%. It's is not happening without an investment, and at WeBank, IT constitutes more than half of the employee base.

China is also pioneering ways to acquire lending customers in a country where few have a credit score. Until a few years ago, only a quarter of the nation's 1.4 billion citizens had a documented credit history.

In the modern era, banks have made lending decisions based on the creditworthiness of the customer or small business. Those with little to no credit history remain shut out of the market.

In response, China's fintech firms began working with the Chinese government to build a social credit score by 2020 – social in this sense is less about whom a person hangs out with and more about the collective, public trust. The Chinese government has said it wants to leverage it in an attempt to foster public confidence and to mitigate corruption. The West has seen it as an ultimate Orwellian surveillance state that raises a host of human rights issues while making the rich richer and the poor poorer. The bottom line in such a vast country? It's not so simple.

In the beginning, the corporate-governmental partnership was about building scores from nontraditional sources of creditworthiness, including social activity, financial literacy quizzes and even games. In 2016, the Brookings Institution reported that "[Alibaba's] Sesame Credit assigns users a score ranging from 350 to 950 based on five criteria: credit history, online transactional habits, personal information, ability to honor an agreement, and social network affiliations. ... Sesame Credit and Tencent Credit draw on the two tech giants' massive pool of user data to assign credit scores, incorporating criteria like a borrower's social network, online shopping history, educational background, income level, and profession."

Then, in 2017, the Chinese government decided that none of the corporate pilots would receive official credit reporting status. It was concerned by potential conflicts of interests. Today, Alibaba's Sesame Credit and Tencent Credit have leveraged their work into larger-scale loyalty programs. Louise Matsakis reported in *WIRED*, "Today, Sesame Credit, as well as other similar initiatives, essentially function like loyalty rewards programs. Participants with high scores earn privileges like renting a bike without leaving a deposit or deferring payment for medical expenses, but the scores are not part of the legal system, and no one is required to participate."

The government has attempted localized pilots, with some even assigning a score, but, as of this writing, it is still very much a work in progress. Nonetheless, in a country with millions of people traditionally denied access to credit, this massive project is one to continue watching.

So, as fintech continues to surge, how can traditional financial institutions go with the flow? Fintech firms have a clear advantage as digital convergence continues.

David Ku, CEO and chairman of WeBank, summarizes its essential structural advantage over traditional banks, saying, "We are essentially a technology company with a banking license, and our growth strategy is powered by ABCD – agility, blockchain, cloud, data."

Might traditional institutions embrace this idea of techfin: technology first and finance later? In the wake of COVID-19, many have been forced to do so. Yet note, traditional banks still have the upper hand. Massive customer bases in a regulated industry help. Brand equity and, in most cases, consumer trust also help. However, and unexpectedly, digital itself is at least buying traditional financial institutions time even as traditional bank deposits are on the move.

Consider this: In 2019, J.D. Power's Retail Banking Satisfaction Study found that just 4% of consumers switched banks in 2018 – the lowest level ever recorded by a research firm. The report noted that it was because of banking convenience. However, *Forbes*' Ron Shevlin vehemently disagrees. He said he believes consumers don't close accounts because money movement is so easy, thanks to digital. Further, he says traditional checking accounts have become "paycheck hotels." Money simply moves to a variety of other digital destinations such as health savings accounts, robo-adviser-based investment accounts and savings accounts through fintech investment upstarts Acorn and Stash. Then it flows through P2P payment apps such as PayPal and Venmo or merchant accounts such as the Starbucks app, where people park money to make purchases. To top it all off, Shevlin says, a recent survey found the following:

"Cornerstone Advisors conducted a survey of 2,393 US consumers between the ages of 21 and 72 who own a smartphone and have a bank account, and asked respondents what they would do if Amazon offered a checking account bundled with other services like cell phone damage protection, ID theft protection, and roadside assistance, for a fee of $5 to $10 a month."

Approximately 40% of 30-something millennials and Gen Xers would make the move. It could represent a loss of $70 billion to $100 billion in deposits.

The traditional financial institution's competitive moat is quickly drying. Time for all such organizations to begin advancing fintech partnerships or acquisitions.

3.4 Autonomous Vehicles:
Digital Drives

Disneyland's Autopia is one of the only park attractions that dates to its opening in 1955. Autopia was designed to honor the future of the American highway – both the freeway and what drove on it. Its first cars were created by a recent graduate from an auto design school and inspired by Porsche and Ferrari.

Autopia's enduring legacy and transformation over the decades illustrate how a technology assimilates into a cultural psyche and holds many touchstones in the heart of consumers, blending a rite of passage, romance, freedom and the power of moving forward. The generational and sentimental tug of the automotive industry is enduring, and many park visitors, particularly from its early days, remember Autopia as one of the first places where they got behind the wheel.

That wheel is transforming, and soon it will not require a driver. Autonomous vehicles are capable of sensing an environment and navigating without human input. It's a space race, and every automaker, parts supplier, tech innovator and ride-share company is in on it. It's converging with other digital trends in the automotive space: the transition from fossil fuel internal combustion engines to battery-powered electrics. Tesla is the poster child for this approach. It has recently surpassed Toyota as the industry's most valuable company and, because of its size and unique approach to selling vehicles, has weathered the COVID-19 outbreak and continues to move ahead, "pedal to the metal."

Its rise comes as a result of sensor technologies and vehicle-to-vehicle connectivity that are fueled by powerful software running on small, relatively inexpensive onboard computers. Like a human driver, autonomous vehicles are constantly scanning the field to answer four key questions: Where am I? What's around me? What will happen next? What should I do?

The extent to which these questions are answered by the vehicle or answered by the driver defines six levels of automation as laid out by the Society of Autonomous Engineers.

Level 1 amounts to driver assistance – the next evolutionary step from cruise control, electronic stability control in inclement weather and lane departure warning, wherein the driver and the automated system in the vehicle share control. At this level, the driver must be prepared to take control of the vehicle at any time. Partial automation arrives at Level 2, wherein the vehicle automation delivers steering and acceleration support that relies on drivers to detect objects and events and respond if the automated system fails to respond appropriately. At Level 3, conditional automation, drivers take control when needed and, within known, limited environments (such as freeways), drivers can safely turn their attention away from driving tasks. With Level 4, high automation, the system takes over all driving functions except for particular environmental concerns, such as when there is severe weather. Level 5, high driving automation, enables the car to be autonomous within a specific zone, such as a "robo-taxi" that works in a geographically limited area. Full automation arrives at Level 6: A vehicle can perform all driving functions autonomously under all conditions. A driver in this type of vehicle does two things: sets a destination and starts the system.

The promise of the autonomous vehicle rests in increasing safety and reducing a lot of things, including collisions, labor costs, insurance costs, energy costs, traffic congestion and pollution. It offers mobility options for those who can't drive or own a car, including the young, the elderly and the socioeconomically disadvantaged who live in areas not served by mass transit. It can also give time back to those who have traditionally spent years behind the wheel commuting.

Though every autonomous vehicle company is striving to achieve Level 6 automation, global consumers are currently only able to purchase Level 2 vehicles. Tesla's "autopilot" offers a perfect example. Audi's AI Traffic Jam Pilot feature was another and was briefly available on the Audi A8 in Europe. This feature enabled the car to operate without driver attention up to 37 mph on certain roads (Level 3). Regulatory complexities to authorize its use on a country-by-country basis in Europe led Audi to pull the feature from the A8 in 2020. Honda is seeking to launch a Level 3 car in 2020 and reach Level 4 by 2025. Google's Waymo project, detailed later in this chapter, has been operating at Level 4 for quite some time. Still, each Waymo vehicle in its "early rider program" includes a test driver in case anything goes wrong. There's a reason for that.

In 2018, the industry was hit hard by a series of safety-related failures. In Arizona, an Uber self-driving car killed a pedestrian. General Motors' self-driving vehicles were involved in six crashes in California, and a motorcyclist sued GM after a collision with an autonomous-driving Chevrolet Bolt.

Naysayers quickly emerged for good reasons, yet it's important to contextualize this negativity against the backdrop of the industry's infancy. At the advent of the horseless carriage in the early 1900s, naysayers were rife and there were significant incidents and accidents.

Critics of the emerging automobile industry primarily focused on the material issues of early automobiles, which were unreliable and inconvenient. For instance, they regularly got stuck in the mud, frequently experienced multiple flat tires a day and required someone to walk in front of them with a red flag in certain cities and towns. Many thought that automobiles would never be more than a novelty. But, with more than 90 million vehicles currently produced each year, these naysayers were clearly wrong.

As automotive manufacturers, technology innovators, auto part suppliers and ride-sharing companies progressively – and inevitably – innovate toward Level 5 and 6 automation, the transport and transportation ecosystem are changing in profound ways. We'll look at four of these changes: ride-sharing fleets, mass transit, long-haul trucking and city planning.

As SAE Level 4 and 5 automation eliminates the need for a driver, it also reduces the need for consumers to purchase personal vehicles. Instead of owning a car, consumers can use on-demand transportation services provided by a group of ride-share companies composed of current players (think Lyft or Uber) and existing car manufacturers.

Rideshares have become increasingly popular in major cities, but they are also gaining traction elsewhere. There are many reasons. First, a typical car in the United States is parked about 95% of the time. Studies have shown that drivers in major cities spend between 17 hours and four days per year looking for a parking space. Ride-shares decrease this waste of time and parking space, and when fully automated, ride-shares enable higher load factors that make the business model even more viable. That business model holds more allure when the total cost of ownership decreases because of the elimination of a driver and translates to increased operating margins in the neighborhood of

20%, which represents double the annual revenue of what carmakers currently generate. Ride-sharing also makes the R&D investment required for Level 5 and 6 automation feasible. Waymo is a case in point. Its Waymo One service is available in Phoenix. Waymo drivers supervise self-driving Chrysler vans, and riders leverage the Waymo app to hail a ride, much like with Uber. An array of ride-sharing fleets would be the best economic structure to support vehicle automation because it provides the lowest cost per mile to consumers.

And there are others, of course. In 2019, GM launched Cruise, a pilot of a self-driving car fleet that is still testing its service in San Francisco. It uses the Chevy Bolt and has unveiled its first driverless vehicle, Origin, which is a vanlike shuttle without a steering wheel or accelerator. Ford plans to launch a fleet of thousands of self-driving cars in 2021. It is this level of market growth that prompted Goldman Sachs to predict that robo-taxis will help the ride-hailing and ride-sharing business grow to $285 billion by 2030.

Mass transit provides another, obvious inroad to autonomous transportation. Just like personal vehicles, it will deliver higher reliability, eventually increased safety and lower costs. Its ability to maximize utilization and minimize congestion will come once on-demand buses embrace dynamic pickup and route schedules. Bus routes based on the real time needs of riders and the mass-transit system will supplant fixed transit routes of most mass-transit systems today. Automated Level 5 and 6 buses are already being tested in several cities, albeit at low speeds.

For example, Denver-based EasyMile 12-person shuttles are being tested in cities throughout the world. Similarly, Japan has introduced driverless buses to shopping centers, airports and university campuses with the goal of using a fleet to connect mass transit to COVID-19-delayed Olympic venues in 2021, and Shenzhen, China, has begun testing self-driving electric minibuses on a 1.2 km loop in the city's Futian District. Importantly, advancements come with fits and starts. In early 2020, the U.S. National Highway Traffic Safety Administration (NHTSA) ordered a fleet of EasyMile shuttles to cease operation after one of them struck a woman in Columbus, Ohio.

Long-haul trucking is also reaping benefit from innovations as a result of Level 4 automation. Compared to passenger cars and mass transit, trucks are driven mostly on open roads and freeways. Even though there are more than 3 million truck drivers in the U.S., long-distance freight trucking costs have increased sharply due to a shortage of drivers and increased safety monitoring. Leading truck and technology players have taken note of the business opportunity. Waymo Via applies the same self-driving technology it's using for its Waymo One service to 18-wheel, Class 8 trucking throughout California and the Southwest. Volvo uses its Vera autonomous trucks to haul stone out of a mine in Norway and is transporting shipping containers to docks in Gothenburg, Sweden. After prototyping automated lorries on public roads in Nevada for three years, Daimler has made a $600 million investment in automated driving features and electric drivetrains and has since expanded testing to Virginia. Meanwhile, Uber is working on a self-driving kit for commercial trucks that will allow drivers to sleep during long-haul trips.

Autonomous transportation is allowing city planners to reimagine the metropolis. It might reverse several trends of the last century: increased vehicle congestion, increased emissions, less use of public transport and increased urban sprawl. Rapid Flow technology, spun up from Carnegie Mellon University's intelligent transportation systems, "optimizes traffic flows every second by adapting to realtime change in traffic." In test conditions, this has led to a 25% reduction in travel times, a 40% reduction in the time spent waiting at signals and a 30% reduction in emissions. Similarly, the Karlsruhe Institute of Technology has conducted simulations that show a lasting 30% reduction in travel times in fully automated traffic.

Where does regulation fit into the automation journey? Earlier, we referenced it in connection with Audi's Traffic Jam Pilot. History tells us that the commercialization of any innovation, especially if human life is at stake, always comes with material regulation and certification requirements.

To date, self-driving efforts on public streets have utilized vehicles that are Federal Motor Vehicle Safety Standards (FMVSS) certified with no material certification or validation of the self-driving technology. As Level 3-6 vehicles become a commercial reality, FMVSS is likely to be amended, with stricter standards for safety, testing and certification.

In the U.S., 22 states and the District of Columbia have already passed legislation allowing testing of autonomous cars on public roads with a back-up driver. In Michigan and California, legislation allows the testing of autonomous cars on public roads. The UK expects to allow fully autonomous vehicle operation in designated areas by 2021 and all over the UK by 2022. Singapore plans to launch an autonomous-exclusive fleet of vehicles no later than 2027. As Level 3-6 vehicles become a commercial reality, it's at the regulatory level that obvious legal, ethical, economic and privacy-related implications of autonomous vehicles will be resolved.

On the ground, autonomous vehicles are forcing several industries to adjust with speed. Automakers will have to reassess their business models and the implications of both decreased sales volume and increased complexity at the intersection of product liability. Shipping and logistics providers will have to remake their infrastructures and emphasize IT and high wage jobs over low cost job categories. Autonomous car rental and ride-sharing will move from an innovative, startup phase into a fierce battle for winning the mainstream. Insurance will feel impacts as product liability becomes the prime risk and fewer cars are parked on streets and in garages. All the while, a new industry around what to do in an autonomous vehicle will blossom, offering inroads to new media-driven experiences and expanding how those experiences are sponsored or underwritten.

As has been repeated many times across technologies and industries within this book, autonomous vehicle adoption is coming – it's a matter of when.

3.5 Government:
Phygital for the People

Wherever you are in the world, full digital is coming to a city near you. Perhaps you've already experienced San Francisco's public parking system that dynamically changes pricing based on occupancy. Maybe your evening in San Diego's Gaslamp District has been lit by one of the city's 3,000 smart streetlights. In New York, you might have made use of one of the city's 7,500 digital kiosks that offer free WiFi, phone calls and device charging. In Oslo, your flat is powered by that city's waste-to-energy conversion system. In Yinchuan, perhaps you've ridden a bus enabled with facial recognition technology that automatically transacts your payment without your having to pay the fare manually. In Bhopal, Kakinada or Jabalpur, you're one of 100 million people residing in one of 100 markets targeted by India's government to transform into a comprehensive "smart city" over the coming years.

Smart cities leverage sensors, networking and artificial intelligence to improve services, conserve resources and engage with citizens. It crosses most categories traditionally associated with city life – transportation, safety and security, utilities, buildings, health care, education, tourism and governance. Today, there nearly 300 smart city initiatives throughout the world, and, over the next two decades, $40 trillion of investment will serve to advance even more.

While budgets, purchasing processes, privacy and cybersecurity are defining the rate and viability of citywide transformations, individualized smart city approaches, as outlined above, are gaining steam because of two primary factors. First, global urbanization is on a fast track, and smart city technologies can ensure this growth happens sustainably. By 2050, 70% of the world population will live in an urban setting. Second, the availability of digital in the form of edge/cloud computing, machine learning, sensors and smartphones is facilitating faster adoption. It means the continued rise in computing power, the lower cost of communication protocols and the miniaturization and diversity of low-cost sensors are making smart city initiatives more accessible and more feasible than ever. Europe and Asia are leading in the retooling effort.

Instrumental to smart city development and planning is AI. As alluded to earlier in fintech, China has seized upon AI and seeks to be its global leader by 2030. As part of the public-private AI partnership to accelerate development and commercialization, the Chinese government has named 15 official governmental partners, including Baidu for autonomous driving; Alibaba for improving urban life and smart transportation; Tencent for computer vision for medical diagnosis; and Huawei for AI infrastructure and software.

Closer to home, the U.S. federal investment in R&D for AI and related technologies has grown significantly over the last five years. In 2019, the U.S. government was set to pour nearly $5 billion into unclassified R&D. At the state level, 64% of state CIOs named AI and machine learning as the most impactful area for them in the next three to five years.

There are four key ways federal, state and city governments are adopting AI: through infrastructure delivery, social and welfare services, national security and law enforcement.

Infrastructure delivery management systems typically include existing core components for planning, supply chain management and asset management. Federal agencies are aggressively using the AI resident in these systems to forecast and recover from natural disasters. The Federal Emergency Management Agency (FEMA) used computer vision analysis of satellite images during the recent and epic Kilauea eruption in Hawaii to determine which buildings had undergone damage and whether people were evacuating ahead of the lava's approach. Additionally, the National Center for Atmospheric Research has recently partnered with IBM Watson to forecast severe weather events more accurately, and thus provide warnings.

While federal agencies have taken the lead, states and cities are not far behind. Maryland has upgraded traffic signals to respond to traffic conditions in real time, with machine-learning-based predictions reducing commute times by 10%-15%. Kansas City can now predict where potholes will form based on past trends, current weather data and existing road conditions. Armed with this information, they can repave streets preemptively before potholes form. Additionally, Chattanooga, Tenn., is using smart grid technology to manage power needs better and mitigate outages during extreme weather.

In social and welfare services, the most significant impact of AI is on education services. The AI investment in U.S. education is expected to grow 48% by 2021 while posting revenues that exceed $25 billion by 2030. In higher education, universities such as Georgia Tech have leveraged AI chatbots to respond to student questions. In Washington state, the Tacoma Public Schools recently partnered with Microsoft on a predictive analytics project to identify students with a high likelihood of dropping out and have seen improvement in graduation rates from 55% to 83%.

Homelessness and child welfare are other issues state and city bodies are tackling through AI. The Center for Innovation through Data Intelligence (CIDI) in the New York City mayor's office uses machine learning to cluster high-risk and formerly homeless individuals using an array of metrics. By measuring frequent jail stays, consistent use of supportive housing or subsidized housing, earlier homeless experience, later homeless experience and minimal welfare service use, the city ascertains critical needs. It also can identify correlative resource requirements. In Europe, the Finnish city of Espoo analyzes 280 factors to predict when families will need child welfare services so that support is offered before serious issues arise.

Federal governments are also using AI across a wide range of overt and covert national security objectives and in support of both public and private enterprises. Military drones and robot soldiers are on the front lines, both in search and rescue and in assisting the military during combat. Intelligence agencies reportedly are supplementing spies with AI to gather information virtually, thus reducing risk to agents. Federal cybersecurity teams are further using AI for intelligence gathering and active threat hunting to "deal with the new wave of sophisticated adversaries."

Vital to national defense is the security support required for critical infrastructure, such as financial institutions and utilities; the federal government has outlined a new cybersecurity policy and set up an infrastructure to respond to virtual attacks.

Law enforcement makes use of AI across its policing activities. In the past, the police would send patrols to historically high crime areas. Using AI tools such as PredPol and CrimeScan, they can predict where crimes will happen and send patrols accordingly; some cities have found AI to be two times better at predicting crime than a human analyst. At crime scenes, police are increasingly using computer-vision-enabled identification technology tied in with body cameras to identify suspects in real time. As police face increasing scrutiny, many of these initiatives have paused. Recently, Amazon implemented a moratorium on police use of its facial recognition technology, Rekognition.

For mass social profiling, perhaps no other government has publicly used AI as extensively as China. China continues to develop its "social credit" system that will be used to rank all citizens dynamically. It intends to predict unwanted behavior, limit freedom of movement, throttle internet speeds, bar citizens from schools or employment and publicly shame individuals as bad citizens.

For obvious reasons, this highlights the more problematic aspects of AI. As in the case of private enterprises, governments have to address two pressing issues in using AI: preventing existing bias in historical data from negatively impacting citizens (especially in military and criminal use cases) and ensuring that users' privacy is not violated through data analysis.

Many governments have already put basic rules and guidelines in place for protections such as privacy, cybersecurity, and health and safety practices. The U.S. government should use these as a starting point to shape the future of AI, hopefully through a "legislation, not regulation" approach. When it comes to protecting citizens' rights, expecting well-meaning private sectors and local governments to self-regulate holds a failing track record.

There are several important implications in all of this for business leaders. First, there is an incredible opportunity for private sector products and services. Governments aren't equipped with the know-how or talent pool to make either happen. Second, smart cities will begin to impact how people choose where they want to live and work.

Third, ongoing urbanization and the impact of COVID-19 will affect how and where companies base their operations and field offices. Finally, as AI and smart city adoption accelerate, cybersecurity and privacy risk exposure increases. Companies partnering with the government must foreground their ability to manage and respond to these risks, and cybersecurity-focused ventures look to win big because of them.

Amid all of this change, there is governance itself. KPMG began offering post-COVID governance perspective as the U.S. was in the throes of a "Phase 2" resurgence. In it, KPMG raises a last point for consideration: "The challenge for digitization is that digitizing the way we do things today releases only limited benefits. In contrast, undertaking fundamental digital transformation to remove unnecessary processes and move to a 'to be' model, can deliver greater effectiveness in terms of improved citizen and workforce experience as well as long-term cost savings."

It's a savvy lead-in signaling that current modes of governance are outdated and based on an industrial-age model. As we move deeper into this century, it means that to upgrade their operating systems, governments worldwide will need to invest in a convergence that enables true phygital for the people.

3.6 Retail:

Shopping Everywhere, One Person at a Time

In May 2020, two months after the United States acknowledged and began to shut down amid the global COVID-19 pandemic, e-commerce sales – already increasing steadily – increased by 93%. In April and May, consumers spent more than $53 billion online. At its center sat Amazon. Its sales were up by 60% between May and July. Amazon claims 38% of the total e-commerce market, and in a distant second place is Walmart, with just 6 percent. *TIME* magazine leverages all of this data to illustrate how crises create opportunities for single-player market dominance:

"Procter & Gamble thrived during the Great Depression by doubling down on advertising; Target expanded after the 2001 recession and saw profits grow 50%. Before the pandemic, Amazon represented around 4% of total U.S. retail sales. But with the new habits formed during the pandemic, UBS predicts that by 2025, e-commerce will make up one-quarter of total retail sales. The firm also estimates that 100,000 brick and mortar retail outlets will close in the next five years."

Brick and mortar, already facing a tsunami, thanks to digital, must confront lasting effects of the pandemic. When you look at this sector in total, it quickly emerges as a critical engine powering the U.S. economy.

PricewaterhouseCoopers and the National Retail Federation annual economic impact report states that retail is responsible for more than 4 million businesses and employs more than 32 million people – one in four Americans. The report, released in May 2020, acknowledges that COVID-19 would directly impact the numbers. Yet it also acknowledges that post-pandemic resilience in retail will be necessary for economic recovery.

For incumbents in this space, digital-convergence-as-tsunami is truly not hyperbole, and brick and mortar leaders have tried to act with speed. To reach second place in the e-commerce category, Walmart has invested billions. It's grown e-commerce sales by 41% and is becoming more poised to take on Amazon.

Other brands have followed suit. Target acquired Shipt to improve its same-day-delivery capabilities, and Nordstrom poured its share of billions into technology investments. Unlike Walmart and Target, Nordstrom has not been an essential business through COVID-19 and, as such, has needed to lean more heavily into its e-commerce wing.

For incumbents that haven't invested primarily in areas such as mobile commerce, personalized marketing and faster distribution have suffered. Six of the top 10 retailers in 1992, as ranked by revenue – Kmart, Sears, American Stores, JC Penney, A&P and May Department Stores – either dropped out of the top 10 after being outpaced by the competition or they've ceased to exist altogether. In 2018, 25 retailers, including the likes of American Apparel, J.Crew, RadioShack, and Toys R Us, filed for bankruptcy or closed a significant number of stores.

There is a blueprint for potential relevance and survival. It rests in meeting consumer expectations. Expectations increasingly set by digital: omnichannel access, the personalization of the shopping experience (as mentioned earlier) and greater immediacy of product.

Today, a given shopper could be purchasing in-store, from an e-commerce destination (again, Amazon, Walmart), a specific consumer brand's website or via click-thru from an Instagram ad. In other words, shoppers are increasingly channel-agnostic, with a desire to engage with brands on their own terms. A study with 46,000 participants showed 73% of shoppers use multiple channels during their shopping journey, while only 7% and 20% are online-only and store-only shoppers, respectively.

Omnichannel – defined as a multichannel approach to sales that seeks to provide customers with a seamless shopping experience, whether they're shopping online from a desktop or mobile device, by telephone or in a brick-and-mortar store – is rapidly becoming the standard operating procedure for thriving brands. The omnichannel trend is most pronounced among millennial shoppers: Nearly half report that they buy online and pickup in-store more than 40% of the time; over half say they switch between buying online and physical stores every week; and nearly a third use retail subscription services. The critical thing to remember? Omnichannel is huge for retailing.

Omnichannel shoppers become more profitable for brands, spending 4% more when shopping in-store and 10% more when shopping online as compared to single-channel shoppers. Businesses have consequently invested in omnichannel capabilities to increase shopper loyalty.

Amazon Prime offered benefits such as free two-day shipping and free same-day delivery to attract over 90 million members, who shop twice as often and spend twice as much as non-Prime members. When Amazon bought Whole Foods, it extended Prime discounts to select products in-store. Restoration Hardware's paid members program, where members pay for perks such as 25% off all full-priced merchandise, account for 95% of the company's core business_while reducing returns and increasing inventory accuracy.

Even as omnichannel opens up points of sale for retail, shoppers also want to feel incredibly unique, looked after. That's where personalization becomes key. According to a McKinsey study, shoppers are looking for five key things: relevant recommendations; communication at the point of being in "shopping mode"; key reminders around most wanted items even if the shopper isn't tracking it; being known as a shopper no matter where interaction takes place; and a sense of shared value in ways that are meaningful to the shopper. Product personalization is also a growing expectation of consumers. According to a Deloitte study, 42% of consumers want technology that enables product customization. Nearly half of that same consumer set is willing to pay up to a 10% premium for that customization.

Retailers are also investing in personalizing the retail experience, with over 70% attempting to merge the "white glove experience of Nordstrom with the data-driven shopping habits of Amazon." Consumers expect more from the brands they purchase and require a compelling reason to visit physical stores. The end-to-end experience is a lynchpin, and consumers are willing to pay more for a better shopping experience.

Brands that can deliver on personalization – that ability to demonstrate knowledge of customer desires and tailor shopping experiences accordingly – have an opportunity to differentiate themselves. While more than half of consumers shop in-store, only one in five shoppers gets the personalized experience he or she is looking for, according to a State of Personalization Report. Brands such as Target have been leading the way with in-store personalization. Target acquired a company called Power Analytics to enable mobile services to personalize the store experience through navigation, recommendations, offers and the accrual of rewards and savings. Online shoppers have set the bar even higher, with more than 75% expecting personalization but finding that only 23% of the stores they shop at deliver on that expectation.

In addition to a richly tailored shopping journey, consumers seek immediate gratification. When they're ready to buy, they want the product immediately. Leading retailers such as Target and Walmart, as well as many vendors on Google Express, have followed Amazon's lead and started offering "free" two-day delivery. While free shipping has become table stakes at this point, with 91% of shoppers saying it would make them a repeat customer, brands are now competing to get consumers what they want as quickly as possible. Same-day shipping is emerging as "ultimate prime."

There's more to immediacy than just speed. Consumers don't want to wait for shipping, and they also expect to be able to find what they want in a physical store. Most check in-store availability online before shopping.

We explored early in this section of the book about how e-commerce firms are going physical to either use their technical prowess to reimagine in-store experiences while expanding market share or solving last-mile distribution challenges. However, some brick and mortar retailers are turning the tables and deepening their ability to leverage the four digital elements we've just discussed.

Best Buy provided a case in point when it made a move to no longer serve as Amazon's "showroom." First, the retailer decided to match any Amazon price on the spot. Second, it has honed simple omnichannel tactics such as buy online/pick up in-store (BOPIS) and surrounded that with a host of convenient services such as in-home setup of entertainment and computer hardware. In turn, it is meeting consumer expectations online while offering a smooth shopping experience – all built upon its brick and mortar brand legacy.

For any incumbent, making a massive and urgent investment in a similar omnichannel experience, personalization and immediacy are now requisite to playing in the age of digital retail. Another brand of distinction in this regard is Nike. To fully leverage the power of digital, Nike has completely reimagined its consumer relationships through a comprehensively connected and thoroughly branded consumer experience. It has invested heavily in a platform that spans physical and digital touchpoints even as it developed an indispensable "logged-in" consumer relationship. It enables the brand to provide truly personalized services at any time or in any place by better understanding consumers' individual needs. When you log in and shop through Nike, you feel seen and known. Over time, it leads to increased purchases.

For all retail – and those who serve it – phygital sells.

3.7 Knowledge Workers:
Phygital Wears a White Collar

Opinion around AI and robotics often assumes the end of so many low-wage, blue-collar jobs. The premise is simple: People who do all sorts of straightforward tasks, from operating machinery to working an assembly line to delivering goods, will have their livelihoods forever altered by automation. In a pre-adoptive phase of AI, this prognostication was based on historical data tied to innovation as a disruptive force that works from the bottom up. Importantly, it does not consider a primary characteristic of AI: its functions "lean" white collar.

The Brookings Institution recently analyzed data modeled by Stanford Ph.D. candidate Michael Webb, who quantified the overlap between AI patent descriptions and white-collar job descriptions. The tool used for this model? AI, of course. The initial results came in and, as Brookings noted:

"The upshot? AI will be a much greater factor in the future work lives of relatively well-paid managers, supervisors, and analysts (as well as production workers, who are increasingly well-educated in many occupations as well as heavily involved with AI on the shop floor). It may be much less of a factor in the work of most, lower-paid service workers."

As we close this book, we'll examine how AI and, in reality, the post-COVID digital acceleration are transforming two entire sectors predominated by white-collar jobs. In both, intuition was leading many firms and individuals to retrain, retool and begin repackaging skill sets to remain something relevant or become something new. The first sector, irresistible and appropriate following our earlier veer into *Mad Men*, is advertising. The second sector emerges in software development – an arena in which software is writing software.

Advertising & Disintermediation

Throughout the first two decades of the 21st century, the advertising industry – particularly old school notions of "ad agencies" – has been proclaimed dead. In this decade, the world's largest ad company, London-headquartered WPP PLC, the parent to agencies such as J. Walter Thompson and Ogilvy & Mather (founded by David Ogilvy, author of the late *Mad Men*-era classic *Ogilvy on Advertising)*, saw a precipitous single-day stock drop. *The Wall Street Journal* reported that "shares in the world's largest advertising company, London-based WPP PLC [owns agencies such as J. Walter Thompson, Young & Rubicam and Ogilvy & Mather], fell nearly 11% ... after it reported a steeper-than-expected slowdown in global ad buying, particularly from consumer-goods companies. It was the stock's biggest one-day drop in more than 18 years. The penny pinching has been widely telegraphed, but the sharp declines at WPP shocked investors." During the COVID pandemic, WPP posted a 3.8% decline in share price in first quarter 2020 alone.

This phenomenon is not limited to WPP. Three others of the Madison Avenue Big Four – Publicis, Interpublic and Omnicom – have seen similar growth challenges. Michael Farmer, an advertising industry veteran, writes in *Madison Avenue Manslaughter*, "What was once one of the most fulfilling and glamorous of industries has become a grim sweatshop for the people who do the work." While that seems like an extreme characterization, it holds some truth, and there is no doubt digital disruption is changing ad agencies.

Ad agencies provide a broad spectrum of services for their clients, including brand positioning and brand strategy creation, creative content strategy and development, media buying, social media strategy and public relations. Typically, revenue comes through a markup on labor and overhead costs for work in any one of the segments mentioned above and, in the case of media buys, a 15% commission across all formats, including print, radio, TV, digital, billboard and cinema. According to WPP's GroupM, the worldwide advertising industry has grown from $493 billion in 2012 to $511 billion in 2017 to a projected $628 billion in 2020. According to *Ad Age*'s coverage of the report, "internet-related advertising is now unambiguously the most important medium globally. TV ad buys will shrink by 3.6 percent. Yet the outlook amid COVID was even bleaker. Google will experience its first-ever ad revenue drop in 2020 since it first "began modeling the business in 2008."

Ad agencies (historically) manage different media buys for their clients. Then they pool their clients' money to negotiate more favorable prices on specific buys. Going to *The New York Times* with five Fortune 500 companies can prove powerful leverage in an industry thirsting for every advertising dollar it can earn. With that "network effect" advantage, an additional fast-growing ad format such as digital should have been a welcome business opportunity. However, the reality is quite the opposite. It's driven by two key factors: disintermediation by digital ad platforms and an inability of agencies to respond to data-based conversion quantification.

The long-foretold moment of disintermediation was ushered in by Google and Facebook. Ad industry growth usually clips along at the 20% range (the pandemic excepted). Google and Facebook captured a stunning 60% of that growth. Like other ad formats, sizeable chunks of digital ad buys from brands continue to go through the money pool paid to agencies. It all began in 2017 when WPP spent $7 billion of total client ad buys with Google and Facebook compared with upward of $2 billion on traditional media. Just five years earlier, Google was the fourth-largest WPP destination for ad spend. Facebook was 28th. However, and importantly, amid this conventional model, an increasing number of brands are going direct. Google and Facebook have made it convenient for advertisers and publishers to interact with advertising marketplaces.

Google started the disintermediation by first building DoubleClick, a marketplace to help buy and sell display advertising. Google followed up with the AdMob platform to help mobile app developers monetize their apps through in-app ads. It further invested in programmatic advertising on both the supply side and the demand side through the DoubleClick bid manager for advertisers to find the right audience. Google advanced DoubleClick for publishers so publishers could find advertisers across all screens. In the meantime, Facebook has built Facebook Audience Network (FAN) to help brands take native ads to third-party publishers. Leveraging the same targeting data used on Facebook or Instagram, it offers easy drop-down menus that identify demographics and psychographics of the people Facebook wants to reach. These platforms provide agency-like functionality. Increasingly, brands are either putting their agency contracts up for review or building in-house agencies that include trading desks. Both moves are either lowering or eliminating marked up billings and the 15% average commission.

Mike Shields illustrates this in a *Business Insider* article dealing with the future of the ad agency: "A few years ago, Booking.com, a hotel e-commerce site owned by Priceline, worked closely with a media-buying agency to figure out where to allocate its ad budgets. 'We'd have meetings where we'd sit down and say, 'We should put this much on YouTube, this much on other sites ...' But Booking.com is about to cut out that middleman, and it could have significant implications for the advertising industry. In recent months, Booking.com has hired data scientists and researchers and other digital-media-buying experts. By the end of the year, all Booking.com's digital-media buying will be done in-house."

Brands today are also keen on data-based conversion quantification. In the past, an ad campaign was deemed "good" if it resonated with the given client or if it was successful with a focus group and then performed reasonably well externally by hitting impression targets. Maybe it also included a call to action that drove website traffic or incited a purchase. Likability and effectiveness of the campaign were neck and neck in the strategic decisioning process.

Google, with its CPC (cost per click) search ads, helped start a mindset change around the quantification of marketing ROI: You could see what people were searching for and clicking. On top of this, brands, through omnichannel approaches to sales and marketing, began making direct, two-way connections with users. Along the way, they gained access to more in-depth consumer demographic and psychographic data than agencies had. As this shift activated, agencies continued to maintain a high-level, gut-leaning creative and campaign mindset. It led Penry Price to write in *Ad Age* that ad agencies urgently needed to act more like technology companies:

"As marketing becomes increasingly driven by data and technology, ad agencies are having to compete for business against a newfound rival:

consulting firms like Accenture and Deloitte......Deloitte has acquired a dozen creative agencies, while Accenture Digital last year was named the largest and fastest-growing digital agency network. Omnicom, for example, created Hearts & Science, an integrated digital agency that uses technology to scale customer relationships. As ad spend continues to shift from TV to digital, agencies will need to hire software engineers, designers and analysts that can quickly build tools and drive the customer experience their clients are looking for. Those that aren't singularly focused on technology to scale the customer experience may find themselves up for review."

These thoughts have given business leaders pause across industries. They are now actively seeking to find an external agency – or build an in-house agency – that combines the right set of skills to help them follow their customers and build meaningful relationships with them across channels. More than ever, they are in a position to understand better who their consumers are, leveraging a full spectrum of data and insights to inform their marketing activities and product development. In particular, CMOs are spending more on IT than CIOs because they know it can ensure empirically sound growth.

It might sound like this shift in strategic capability and analysis would prove insurmountable for ad agencies. Are their days finally numbered? Like fintech, tech-first and user-relationship-meets-experience focused agencies or niche-owning agencies (e.g., creative, search, mobile and social) will find their way. Amid this shift, one could argue that the end is nigh for legacy agency super-firms such as WPP and Publicis. However, history has demonstrated that their agility, creativity and adaptability prove once again that Don Draper would find a way to coexist with the IBM System/360.

Software Writing Software

Shifting from *Mad Men*, let's turn to another episodic series – the HBO comedy series *Silicon Valley*. In a 2019 season six episode, the main character, Gilfoyle, asks his AI to find a cheap burger on his way to facilitating an officewide lunch. Soon, 4,000 pounds of raw beef is delivered. Here, AI plays the goofy, bumbling sidekick.

In many ways, AI is still relatively new, but it is far from bumbling. IDC has claimed that, at this point, it is inescapable. It devours large sets of data, and when the proper algorithm is applied, it can learn, it can act and react, and it can answer "how" and "what" questions with great ferocity. All of this capability has been put to use, and AI is now writing software. It, too, is in its nascent stages, but it's beginning to take hold.

Software writing software shouldn't be that much of a surprise. Our lives are becoming increasingly software-enabled. The last 20 years have seen more than 1 billion websites and 3 million apps launch on iOS and Android combined. Along the way, digital is driving and reshaping what's called the technology stack – the blend of software products and programming languages used to create a web or mobile application (app).

In 2017, *New Scientist* reported that "Microsoft and the University of Cambridge have created a system [called DeepCoder] that could allow non-coders to simply describe an idea for a program and let the system build it [by] piecing together lines of code taken from existing software – just like a programmer might."

That same year, *WIRED* reported that "Google's researchers have taught machine-learning software [AutoML] to build machine-learning software. ... [For] marking the location of multiple objects in an image, the auto-generated system scored 43 percent. The best human-built system scored 39 percent."

In 2019, two MIT professors, Armando Solar-Lezama and Josh Tenenbaum, developed SketchAdapt, which can learn to "compose short, high-level programs while letting the second set of algorithms find the right sub-programs to fill in the details." What makes it intriguing is that "it knows when to switch from statistical pattern-matching to a less efficient, but more versatile, symbolic reasoning mode to fill in the gaps." It's already outperformed DeepCoder.

The most significant impact of software writing software is the realignment of developers within the enterprise, and it's worthy of attention. If you're reading this and think it spells the demise of the programmer, note that a very early programming language known as FORTRAN (aka the FORTRAN Automatic Coding System) was developed in the 1950s with the expectation that it would replace human developers. With more than 23 million software developers worldwide as of 2018, Fortran did not win.

Importantly, within the SketchAdapt example, its developers have positioned it to "complement human programmers." It enables people to tell the intelligent machine what they want, and the intelligent machine takes it from there. IT highlights how the role of the developer will change from a step-by-step, from-scratch rules-oriented engineer to an agile maestro. Next-generation developers will possess a skill set focused on a thorough understanding around maximizing the cloud and public APIs. It will be equipped to steward application development and delivery (AD&D) automation, which eliminates software upgrades and replaces them with real time, machine-learning-derived tweaks. They will have a firm grounding in data-driven programming that knows how to manipulate software written by software that backs computer vision, self-driving cars, chatbots and speech translation.

As Jensen Huang, CEO of NVIDIA, has aptly summarized it, "AI is eating software!" Maybe as a phrase, it's not as poetic as "culture eats strategy for breakfast," but it underscores how AI, the big data it requires and the speed with which it learns and attunes itself, is a big deal for the future of software development.

Importantly, there is a need to underscore that while AI applied to software is filled with the benefits derived from automation and efficiency, it cannot yet secure differentiation. That will continue to come from strategically thoughtful, visionary and fully integrated end-to-end customer experiences. It takes human craftsmanship to array "best in class" technology solutions elegantly to deliver any unique experience.

I've purposefully ended this book with this chapter for a reason. Digital is about transformation and evolution – not the end of anything. Jobs, careers, lives and how we live them will still depend on us – our resourcefulness and our agility to navigate and flourish in the digital future. As noted historian Arthur Schlesinger Jr. said, "Science and technology revolutionize our lives, but memory, tradition and myth frame our response."

Epilogue

Every business has become or is transitioning into a digital business. We live in a world where the forces shaping this digital revolution are often challenging to understand. I hope that, having read this book, you are better equipped to frame and leverage digital power as you make strategic decisions within your company, career and life. To explore the intelligent machine, the technology it fosters and multiplies and the way it converges at philosophical and industrial levels is a digital transformation unto itself. Armed with this knowledge, what should you consider as a next step?

Act. Now.

Now is the time to equal digital's breakneck pace. Not even COVID-19 can stop it; it may even accelerate it. The giants of digital are proving as much. Through COVID, Amazon doubled its net profit, year-over-year, from $2.6 billion to $5.2 billion. Facebook's second quarter 2020 revenue was up 11% to $18.7 billion, and net profit had increased by 98% to $5.2 billion. In the same quarter, Ford Motor Co. outperformed a forecasted loss. Why? Its investment in Argo AI, an autonomous driving company, experienced a gain in value from which Ford earned $1.1 billion. These numbers align with and cue the Law of Accelerating Returns (LOAR) we touched on in Part 1.

Waxing more specific, now is the time for swift, bold moves to lead, to establish policy and to hammer out governance concerning digital today, even as we anticipate where it will head tomorrow. What follows are five high-level issues upon which these moves should focus.

First, incumbents must recast their entire organization in terms of digital. Either they will lead with digital, or they will perish. Throughout Part 3, we explored the strategic and tactical approaches to digital that have equipped incumbents for a successful recast. By using established physical infrastructure, distribution advantages, unrivaled customer bases and unique avenues into consumer experiences, incumbents can employ digital to amplify their trajectories. It requires massive investment in digital capabilities that includes unprecedented shifts to ensure digitally fluent talent across the enterprise. That means moving beyond a dedicated digital team to a digital mindset shared by the board of directors, CEO, senior leadership and the rank and file.

Second, as the digital cold war escalates, companies must consider how they will evaluate and conduct digital business across borders. Set off by the intensifying trade war between the United States and China in 2019, this new cold war is fracturing the very nature of the internet. The splinternet – alternative, parallel internets marked by "market-open" communism and free-market capitalism – is quickly taking shape. China has blocked Google, Twitter and several apps it deems a threat to its national security. The U.S. and nearly all of the 70 nations in the Organization for Economic Cooperation and Development are either banning or pushing back hard on Huawei's 5G infrastructure mission. India recently banned 59 Chinese apps because of differing views on privacy intrusions. As of this writing, TikTok's future in the U.S. is uncertain – though Microsoft may acquire its U.S. operations. These aren't merely decisions that set the tone for international commerce.

They are geopolitical battles for a digital future that is creating two distinct internets with distinctly different rules. It's already impacted how companies look at total available market (TAM) that results when a global pie gets sliced between U.S.- and China-centric opportunities. We know that 5G could be the single-most-defining battle of the early 21st century, and right now it's pitted Western players versus Huawei in a quest to win country-by-country adoption. Alongside it is a reconfiguration of supply chains as U.S. and other allied countries seek ways to shift as much as possible out of China. In turn, China is sprinting to become domestically self-sufficient.

On top of this, data is getting walled in by sovereign nations, creating complexities around cross-border information flow that impact who uses what apps and where. Finally, multinationals are evaluating their public-facing brands connected to corporate values, social justice, human rights and all sorts of ways in which business practices could help or harm business in diverse political milieus. In response, organizations must quickly grasp and analyze the digital cold war's ramifications on their current industry-based contexts and business models, adjusting accordingly.

Third, in digital, the current business environment favors returns-to-scale oriented companies that could threaten consumer-beneficial competition throughout the digital landscape. There are rare bipartisan concerns in Congress around "big tech" and its power. Amazon, Facebook, Google and Apple CEOs testified to a House antitrust subcommittee to defend charges of potentially anti-competitive practices. In Part 2, we touched on big data as the new oil. And just like with oil, steel and tobacco, age-old questions of how to balance patent and intellectual property protection against the risk of outright monopolies have reignited. It means federal and state governments must become digitally aware to ensure that thoughtful, circumspect legislation wins the day over hastily established regulatory constraints that could threaten global digital relevance.

Fourth, data in its totality must be addressed and handled with care and vigilance. National, regional and individual security are at stake. For this, cybersecurity and national preparedness for cyberattacks must increase even as cyberattack elegance advances. Deepfakes illustrate new levels of attack sophistication. Deepfakes are AI-generated video and audio that could stoke civil conflict through the spread of disinformation. MIT's Center for Advanced Virtuality recently demonstrated as much by manipulating footage of Richard Nixon, creating a deepfake featuring the president delivering a speech announcing that the Apollo 11 moon landing ended in disaster. The imagery, mannerisms and voice are all true to Nixon.

Companies must also consider where their data travels in the splinternet age. Zoom recently admitted to accidentally routing through China some meetings and digitally encrypted keys designed to maintain meeting confidentiality. Chinese regulations give its government the power to seize secret access to those keys no matter where the meeting took place geographically. Data flow, then, must be planned and mapped with a premium placed on safety.

As AI modeling expands and becomes applied across society, its inherent bias through the data used to train it must be acknowledged and definitively addressed. Bias can come in the form of human decisions and includes historical or social inequities. Strong public-private partnerships and new levels of ethical leadership tied to eliminating bias will begin to solve this issue.

Finally, companies must account for new jobs, evolving jobs and the skills required for both in the new digital reality. This last issue has a lineage worth discussing. Consider the Luddite cause. When we think Luddite today, we picture individuals who are particularly tech-avoidant – laggards. Two centuries ago, Luddites were British citizens facing economic upheaval against the backdrop of industrial change. They attacked the machines they worked on not because they were against technology but because food and work were scarce and jobs didn't pay enough.

We face that same issue today. Our workforce isn't against digital – workers use it all day, every day. However, we need an educational revolution that can keep companies and their workers digitally current, no matter the industry. To do so would require, at a minimum, curricula grounded in science, technology, engineering and mathematics (STEM) and a wholly reframed approach to self-education in corporate environments that would ensure marketplace-relevant skills throughout an individual's full professional life.

This last point – self-education – brings this book full circle. It is the journey you have made. If you're a corporate leader, it's a journey your entire organization should make. Act now. In that, I wish you well.

Notes

1.1 Storage: The Story of Memory

Cornish, Chloe. (2018). How DNA Could Store All the World's Data in a Semi-Trailer. Financial Times. Retrieved online: ft.com/content/45ea22b0-cec2-11e7-947e-f1ea5435bcc7

Morgan, Steve. (2020). The World Will Store 200 Zettabytes of Data by 2025. Cybercrime Magazine. Retrieved online: cybersecurityventures.com/the-world-will-store-200-zettabytes-of-data-by-2025

Roberts, Fran. (2020). IBM Achieves New World Record in Magnetic Tape Storage. Technology Magazine. Retrieved online: technologymagazine.com/big-data/ibm-achieves-new-world-record-magnetic-tape-storage

1.2 Computing: The Story of Speed

Anthony, Sebastian. (2017). IBM Unveils First 5nm Chip. Ars Technica. Retrieved online: arstechnica.com/gadgets/2017/06/ibm-5nm-chip

Bell, Lee. (2016). What is Moore's Law? WIRED Explains the Theory That Defined the Tech Industry. WIRED. Retrieved online: wired.co.uk/article/wired-explains-moores-law

Federowicz, Evan. (2020). Samsung Makes the First 3nm GAAFET Semiconductor! WCCFTech. Retrieved Online: wccftech.com/samsung-makes-the-first-3nm-gaafet-semiconductor

1.3 Software: The Story of Digital Self-Expression

Dediu, Horace. (2012). How Much Do Maps Cost and How Much Are They Worth? Asymco.com. Retrieved online: asymco.com/2012/12/18/how-much-to-maps-cost-and-what-are-they-worth

Doyle, Brandon. (2020). TikTok Statistics – Updated August 2020. Wallaroo Media. Retrieved online: wallaroomedia.com/blog/social-media/tiktok-statistics

Geer, David. (2019). API Security Lives at the Heart of the Breach. Threat X Labs. Retrieved online: blog.threatxlabs.com/api-security-lives-at-the-heart-of-the-breach

Iyer, Bala and Subramaniam, Mohan. (2015) The Strategic Value of APIs. Harvard Business Review. Retrieved online: hbr.org/2015/01/the-strategic-value-of-apis

Murphy, Matt and Sloane, Steve. (2016). The Rise of APIs. TechCrunch. Retrieved online: techcrunch.com/2016/05/21/the-rise-of-apis

1.4 Connecting: The Story of Digital Contact

Sources for the speed of connectivity across wired, mobile and wired innovations appear courtesy the Broadband World Forum, IEEE and Qualcomm.

Campbell, Charlie. (2019). Inside the Controversial Company Helping China Control the Future of the Internet. TIME magazine. Retrieved online: time.com/5594366/5g-internet-race-huawei

Weaver, Bridgett. (2018). AT&T to Launch 5G Coverage in Louisville. Louisville Business First. Retrieved online: bizjournals.com/louisville/news/2018/09/10/at-t-to-launch-5g-coverage-in-louisville.html

1.5 Sensing: The Story of Deeper Data and Greater Acuity

Sources for the camera comparison appear courtesy Canon and Apple.

Phelan, David. (2019). Movie Shot on iPhone by Oscar-Winning Director Premieres at Cannes. Forbes. Retrieved online: forbes.com/sites/davidphelan/2019/05/25/movie-shot-on-iphone-from-oscar-winning-director-premieres-at-cannes-film-festival-filmic-pro

1.6 The Machine in Full: The Five Building Blocks and LOAR

Multifactor growth numbers across building blocks appear courtesy iMore.com and everymac.com.

Kurzweil, Raymond. (2001). The Law of Accelerating Returns. Retrieved online: kurzweilai.net/the-law-of-accelerating-returns

2.1 Big Data: The New Oil

(2014). Federal Trade Commission. Data Brokers: A Call for Transparency and Accountability. Retrieved online: ftc.gov/reports/data-brokers-call-transparency-accountability-report-federal-trade-commission-may-2014

(2019). IDC. The Growth in Connected IoT Devices Is Expected to Generate 79.4ZB of Data in 2025, According to a New IDC Forecast. Retrieved online: idc.com/getdoc.jsp?containerId=prUS45213219

Ali, Umar. (2019). The History of the Oil and Gas Industry from 347 AD to today. Offshore Technology. Retrieved online: offshore-technology.com/comment/history-oil-gas

Balakumar, K. (2020). U.S. Continues to Back Jio on 5G Tech. TechRadar. Retrieved online: techradar.com/news/us-continues-to-back-jio-on-5g-tech

Dawar, Niraj. (2017). Has Google Finally Proven That Online Ads Cause Offline Purchases? Harvard Business Review. Retrieved online: hbr.org/2017/06/has-google-finally-proven-that-online-ads-cause-offline-purchases

Gill, Prabhjote. (2020). Mukesh Ambani AGM Speech Highlights – Reliance Industries Announces Jio Glass, Google Partnership and Plans to Build a New Smartphone. Business Insider India. Retrieved online: businessinsider.in/business/corporates/news/checkout-mukesh-ambani-reliance-industries-annual-general-meeting-highlights/articleshow/76976243.cms

Kitchin, Rob. (2014). The Data Revolution: Big Data, Open Data, Data Infrastructures and Their Consequences. SAGE: Thousand Oaks, Calif.

Sterling, Greg. (2019). Almost 70% of Digital Ad Spending Going to Google, Facebook, Amazon, Says Analyst Firm. Marketing Land. Retrieved online: marketingland.com/almost-70-of-digital-ad-spending-going-to-google-facebook-amazon-says-analyst-firm-262565

2.2 Cloud: Digital Power from Afar

(2017). Classified Pentagon Data Leaked on the Public Cloud. BBC. Retrieved online: bbc.com/news/technology-42166004

(2019). IDC. The Growth in Connected IoT Devices Is Expected to Generate 79.4ZB of Data in 2025, According to a New IDC Forecast. Retrieved online: idc.com/getdoc.jsp?containerId=prUS45213219

(2020). Global Cloud Infrastructure Services Market by Manufacturers, Countries, Type and Application, Forecast to 2025. MarketsandResearch.biz. Retrieved online: marketsandresearch.biz/report/11226/global-cloud-infrastructure-services-market-by-manufacturers-countries-type-and-application-forecast-to-2025

(2020). Top 8 Cloud Outages That Shook the Tech World in 2020. Senseclouds. Retrieved online: senseclouds.com/blog/2019/12/top-8-cloud-outages-that-shook-the-tech-world-in-2020

Sanders, James and Forrest, Conner. (2014). Hybrid Cloud: What It Is, Why It Matters. ZDNet. Retrieved online: zdnet.com/article/hybrid-cloud-what-it-is-why-it-matters

King, Rachael. (2017). Dell Bets $1 Billion on Internet of Things. The Wall Street Journal. Retrieved online: wsj.com/articles/dell-bets-1-billion-on-internet-of-things-1507647601

Postman, Neil. (1993). Technopoly: The Surrender of Culture to Technology. Vintage Books: New York.

Rouse, Margaret. (Updated 2020). What is Cloud Migration? An Introduction to Moving to the Cloud. TechTarget. Retrieved online: searchcloudcomputing.techtarget.com/definition/cloud-migration

Van der Meulen, Rob. (2018). What Edge Computing Means for Infrastructure and Operations Leaders. Gartner. Retrieved online: gartner.com/smarterwithgartner/what-edge-computing-means-for-infrastructure-and-operations-leaders

2.3 Cybersecurity: Threats, Protection and Response

For information on e-Estonia, visit e-estonia.com.
(2017). ITRC Data Breach Reports. PDF retrieved online: idtheftcenter.org/images/breach/2017Breaches/DataBreach Report_2017.pdf

Chin, Josh and Wong, Gillian. (2016). China's New Tool for Social Control: A Credit Rating for Everything. The Wall Street Journal. Retrieved online: wsj.com/articles/chinas-new-tool-for-social-control-a-credit-rating-for-everything-1480351590

Cook, James. (2014). JP Morgan Got Hacked Because It Forgot To Enable Two-Factor Authentication on a Server. Business Insider. Retrieved online: businessinsider.com/jp-morgan-hacked-because-it-forgot-two-factor-authentication-2014-12

Irwin, Luke. (2019). New Orleans is the Latest City Crippled by Ransomware Attack. IT Governance. Retrieved online: itgovernanceusa.com/blog/new-orleans-is-the-latest-city-crippled-by-ransomware

Larson, Selena. (2018). Major Chip Flaws Affect Billions of Devices. CNN. Retrieved online: money.cnn.com/2018/01/03/technology/computer-chip-flaw-security/index.html

Mathews, Lee. (2017). Equifax Data Breach Impacts 143 Million Americans. Forbes. Retrieved online: forbes.com/sites/leemathews/2017/09/07/equifax-data-breach-impacts-143-million-americans

Sanger, David E., Kirkpatrick, David D. and Perlroth, Nicole. (2017). The World Once Laughed at North Korean Cyberpower. No More. The New York Times. Retrieved online: nytimes.com/2017/10/15/world/asia/north-korea-hacking-cyber-sony.html

Schmidhuber, Jurgen. (2017). Falling Walls: The Past, Present and Future of Artificial Intelligence. Scientific American. Retrieved online: blogs.scientificamerican.com/observations/falling-walls-the-past-present-and-future-of-artificial-intelligence

Sienko, Chris. (Undated). The Breach of Anthem Health – The Largest Healthcare Breach in History. Infosec Institute. Retrieved online: resources.infosecinstitute.com/category/healthcare-information-security/healthcare-attack-statistics-and-case-studies/case-study-health-insurer-anthem

Swearingen, Jake. (2018). Nearly Every Computer Made Since 1995 Is Dangerously Flawed. Here's What You Need to Know. New York Magazine. nymag.com/intelligencer/2018/01/intel-chip-security-flaw-meltdown-spectre-what-to-know-explainer.html

Vijayan, Jaikumar. (2014). Target Attack Shows Danger of Remotely Accessible HVAC Systems. ComputerWorld. Retrieved online: computerworld.com/article/2487452/target-attack-shows-danger-of-remotely-accessible-hvac-systems.html

Williamson, Wade. (2014). What Happens to Stolen Data After a Breach? SecurityWeek. Retrieved online: securityweek.com/what-happens-stolen-data-after-breach

Winder, Davey. (2019). The Top 10 Cybersecurity Stories of 2019 – A Window onto the 2020 Threatscape. Forbes. Retrieved online: forbes.com/sites/daveywinder/2019/12/27/the-top-10-cybersecurity-stories-of-2019-a-window-onto-the-2020-threatscape

2.4 Artificial Intelligence: The Opportunity of Pandora

Deeper information on Santiago Ramón y Cajal is available at nobelprize.org

Goode, Lauren. (2018). Google CEO Sundar Pichai Compares Impact of AI to Electricity and Fire. The Verge. Retrieved online: theverge.com/2018/1/19/16911354/google-ceo-sundar-pichai-ai-artificial-intelligence-fire-electricity-jobs-cancer

Kats, Rimma. (2018). Why Isn't Everyone Living in an AR/VR World? eMarketer. Retrieved online: emarketer.com/content/why-isn-t-everyone-living-in-an-ar-vr-world

Kelly, Kevin. (2014). The Three Breakthroughs That Have Finally Unleashed AI on the World. WIRED. Retrieved online: wired.com/2014/10/future-of-artificial-intelligence

Marr, Bernard. (2018). The Key Definitions of Artificial Intelligence (AI) That Explain Its Importance. Forbes. Retrieved online: forbes.com/sites/bernardmarr/2018/02/14/the-key-definitions-of-artificial-intelligence-ai-that-explain-its-importance

Noë, Alva. (2017). The Art of the Brain, On Exhibit. NPR. Retrieved online: npr.org/sections/13.7/2017/01/20/510528975/the-art-of-the-brain-on-exhibit

Prakash, Abishur. (2018). Facial Recognition Cameras and AI: 5 Countries with the Fastest Adoption. Robotics Business Review. Retrieved online: roboticsbusinessreview.com/ai/facial-recognition-cameras-5-countries

Purdy, Mark and Daugherty, Paul. (2017). How AI Boosts Industry Profits and Innovation. Accenture. Retrieved online: accenture.com/t20170620T055506_w_/us-en/_acnmedia/Accenture/next-gen-5/insight-ai-industry-growth/pdf/Accenture-AI-Industry-Growth-Full-Report.pdf

Puiu, Tibi. (2017). How Big is a Petabyte, Exabyte or Yottabyte? What's the Biggest Byte for That Matter? ZME Science. Retrieved online: zmescience.com/science/how-big-data-can-get

Sharma, Manimugdha S. (2019). Hindu Epics Are Full of AI, Robots. Legend Has It That They Guarded Buddha's Relics. The Times of India. Retrieved online: timesofindia.indiatimes.com/home/sunday-times/all-that-matters/hindu-epics-are-full-of-ai-robots-legend-has-it-that-they-guarded-buddhas-relics/articleshow/68648962.cms

Shashkevich, Alex. (2019). Stanford Researcher Examines Earliest Concepts of Artificial Intelligence, Robots in Ancient Myths. Stanford.edu. Retrieved online: news.stanford.edu/2019/02/28/ancient-myths-reveal-early-fantasies-artificial-life

Simonite, Tom. (2017). Apple's 'Neural Engine' Infuses the iPhone With AI Smarts. WIRED. Retrieved online: wired.com/story/apples-neural-engine-infuses-the-iphone-with-ai-smarts

Suvarna, Hitesh. (2017). Hinduism, Evolution & Artificial Intelligence. Medium.com. Retrieved online: medium.com/@hitesh.suvarna666/hinduism-evolution-artificial-intelligence-6c56fcb0e736

Vincent, James. (2017). Facebook is Using AI to Spot Users with Suicidal Thoughts and Send Them Help. The Verge. Retrieved online: theverge.com/2017/11/28/16709224/facebook-suicidal-thoughts-ai-help

2.5 Augmented & Virtual Reality: Digital's Alternative Universe

For more on the Philadelphia Orchestra's augmented reality app, visit youtube.com/watch?v=5qr4xTje6RA

Castellanos, Sara. (2018). Lockheed Martin Deploys Augmented Reality for Spacecraft Manufacturing. The Wall Street Journal. Retrieved online: blogs.wsj.com/cio/2018/08/01/lockheed-martin-deploys-augmented-reality-for-spacecraft-manufacturing

Dujmovic, Jurica. (2019). Opinion: Here's Why You Will be Hearing More About Virtual Reality. MarketWatch. Retrieved online: marketwatch.com/story/heres-why-you-will-be-hearing-more-about-virtual-reality-2019-07-15

Dowsett, Sonya. (2018). Zara to Lure Millennials with Augmented-Reality Displays. Reuters. Retrieved online: reuters.com/article/us-inditex-zara-technology/zara-to-lure-millennials-with-augmented-reality-displays-idUSKCN1GP2TC

Gownder, J.P. (2016). How Enterprise Smart Glasses Will Drive Workforce Enablement. Forrester. Retrieved online: forrester.com/report/How+Enterprise+Smart+Glasses+Will+Drive+Workforce+Enablement/-/E-RES133722

Madnani, Mikhail. (2016). A Brief History of Pokémon. livemint. Retrieved online: livemint.com/Sundayapp/Z7zHxltyWtFNzcoXPZAbjI/A-brief-history-of-Pokmon.html
Merel, Tim. (2018). Ubiquitous AR to Dominate Focused VR by 2022. TechCrunch. Retrieved online: techcrunch.com/2018/01/25/ubiquitous-ar-to-dominate-focused-vr-by-2022

Vincent, Brittany. (2018). 'Pokémon Go' Celebrates Two-Year Anniversary With $1.8 Billion Revenue Milestone. Variety. Retrieved online: variety.com/2018/gaming/news/pokemon-go-2-years-1-billion-1202867409

2.6 Digital Currency: Trading Trust for a Puzzle

The history of gold appears courtesy the National Mining Association. For more, visit nma.org/pdf/gold/gold_history.pdf

The history of Bitcoin appears courtesy its Wikipedia entry at en.wikipedia.org/wiki/History_of_bitcoin

Current Bitcoin market cap is available at statista.com/statistics/377382/bitcoin-market-capitalization
O'Connor, Matt R. (2016). Can Bitcoin Be Gold 2.0? Seeking Alpha. Retrieved online: seekingalpha.com/article/3964321-can-bitcoin-be-gold-2_0

Posner, Eric. (2013). Fool's Gold. Slate. Retrieved online: slate.com/news-and-politics/2013/04/bitcoin-is-a-ponzi-scheme-the-internet-currency-will-collapse.html

2.7 Sans Display: The Post-Screen IoT World

(2017). Alexa, Say What?! Voice-Enabled Speaker Usage to Grow Nearly 130% This Year. eMarketer. Retrieved online: emarketer.com/Article/Alexa-Say-What-Voice-Enabled-Speaker-Usage-Grow-Nearly-130-This-Year/1015812

Kemp, Simon. (2019). Digital 2019: Global Internet Use Accelerates. We Are Social. Retrieved online: wearesocial.com/blog/2019/01/digital-2019-global-internet-use-accelerates

Part 3 Phygital: Where Worlds Converge

Borowski, Craig. (2015). What a Great Digital Customer Experience Actually Looks Like. Harvard Business Review. Retrieved online: hbr.org/2015/11/what-a-great-digital-customer-experience-actually-looks-like

Bort, Julie. (2016). Netflix Exec Explains the Simple But Painful Process That Allows the Company to Thrive. Business Insider. Retrieved online: businessinsider.com/how-netflix-recreates-itself-2016-9

Hopkins, Brian. (2016). Forrester's Top Emerging Technologies to Watch: 2017-2021. Forrester. Retrieved online: go.forrester.com/blogs/16-09-14-forresters_top_emerging_technologies_to_watch_2017_2021

Tung, Hans. (2017). Beyond Amazon and Alibaba: What's Next for E-commerce? TechCrunch. Retrieved online: techcrunch.com/2017/08/20/beyond-amazon-and-alibaba-whats-next-for-e-commerce

3.1 Convergence: Shifting Reality

For a complete overview of the ride-sharing vs. taxi legal history, visit: en.wikipedia.org/wiki/Legality_of_ridesharing_companies_by_jurisdiction

Goodwin, Tom. (2015). The Battle is for the Customer Interface. TechCrunch. Retrieved online: techcrunch.com/2015/03/03/in-the-age-of-disintermediation-the-battle-is-all-for-the-customer-interface

Liffreing, Ilyse. (2017). Why E-commerce Brands are Flipping the Script and Opening Brick-and-Mortar Stores. DigiDay. Retrieved online: digiday.com/marketing/e-commerce-brands-opening-brick-mortar-stores

Lessin, Sam. (2020). The Escalating War Between Our Physical and Digital Realities. The Information. Retrieved online: theinformation.com/articles/the-escalating-war-between-our-physical-and-digital-realities

Locker, Melissa. (2017). Airbnb Denounces Hotel-backed NYC Sting Operations as "Second-Rate KGB Spy Tactics." Fast Company. Retrieved online: fastcompany.com/4043212/airbnb-denounces-hotel-backed-nyc-sting-operations-as-second-rate-kgb-spy-tactics

Thompson, Derek. (2017). Why Amazon Bought Whole Foods. The Atlantic. Retrieved online: theatlantic.com/business/archive/2017/06/why-amazon-bought-whole-foods/530652

Wille, Matthew. (2020). Spotify Appears to Be Testing a Smart Speaker Called "Home Thing." Input. Retrieved online: inputmag.com/tech/spotify-appears-to-be-testing-a-smart-speaker-called-home-thing

3.2 Health Care and Pharma: Frictionless Care and Greater Transparency

For a complete overview of the Merritt Hawkins survey of physician appointment wait times, visit: merritthawkins.com/news-and-insights/thought-leadership/survey/survey-of-physician-appointment-wait-times

Accenture's patient engagement report is available at accenture.com/t20170412t073547z_w_/us-en/_acnmedia/pdf-6/accenture-patient-engagement-digital-self-scheduling-explode.pdf

DiMasi, Joseph A., Grabowski, Henry G. and Hansen, Ronald W. (2016). Innovation in the Pharmaceutical Industry: New Estimates of R&D Costs. Elsevier. Retrieved online: sciencedirect.com/science/article/abs/pii/S0167629616000291

Dyrda, Laura. (2020). Haven Has Been Quiet for the Past Two Years – What Does That Mean for Healthcare? Becker's Health IT. Retrieved online: beckershospitalreview.com/healthcare-information-technology/haven-has-been-quiet-for-the-past-2-years-what-does-that-mean-for-healthcare.html

Landi, Heather. (2019). CVS Health Exec: Retail Giant Wants to Create a Netflix-like Healthcare Experience. Fierce Healthcare. Retrieved online: fiercehealthcare.com/tech/cvs-health-s-digital-executive-we-want-to-create-a-healthcare-experience-as-easy-to-use-and

LaVito, Angelica. (2018). CVS Creates New Health-Care Giant as $69 billion Merger with Aetna Officially Closes. CNBC. Retrieved online: cnbc.com/2018/11/28/cvs-creates-new-health-care-giant-as-69-billion-aetna-merger-closes.html

Wingfield, Nick, Thomas, Katie and Abelson, Reed. (2018). Amazon, Berkshire Hathaway and JPMorgan Team Up to Try to Disrupt Health Care. The New York Times. Retrieved online: nytimes.com/2018/01/30/technology/amazon-berkshire-hathaway-jpmorgan-health-care.html

Wouters, Olivier J., McKee, Martin and Luyten, Jeroen. (2020). Estimated Research and Development Investment Needed to Bring a New Medicine to Market, 2009-2018. JAMA Network. Retrieved online: jamanetwork.com/journals/jama/article-abstract/2762311

Thorlund, Kristian, Dron, Louis, Park, Jay, Hsu, Grace, Forrest, Jamie I. and Mills, Edward J. (2020). A Real-Time Dashboard of Clinical Trials for COVID-19. The Lancet. Retrieved online: thelancet.com/journals/landig/article/PIIS2589-7500(20)30086-8/fulltext

3.3 Financial Services: Money Transformed

To track the number of banks in China between 2009 and 2017, visit: statista.com statistics/259910/number-of-banks-in-china

For a complete picture of China's GDP, visit: tradingeconomics.com/china/gdp

For the PricewaterhouseCoopers perspective on fintech, visit: pwc.com/gx/en/industries/financial-services/publications/fintech-is-reshaping-banking.html

Matsakis, Louis. (2019). How the West Got China's Social Credit System Wrong. WIRED. Retrieved online: wired.com/story/china-social-credit-score-system

Mozur, Paul. (2017). In Urban China, Cash Is Rapidly Becoming Obsolete. The New York Times. Retrieved online: nytimes.com/2017/07/16/business/china-cash-smartphone-payments.html?mcubz=1

Shevlin, Ron. (2019). An Amazon Checking Account Could Displace $100 Billion In Bank Deposits (But It Won't). Forbes. Retrieved online: forbes.com/sites/ronshevlin/2019/01/21/an-amazon-checking-account-could-displace-250-billion-in-bank-deposits-but-it-wont

Wang, Wei and Dollar, David. (2018). What's Happening with China's Fintech Industry? Brookings Institution. Retrieved online: brookings.edu/blog/order-from-chaos/2018/02/08/whats-happening-with-chinas-fintech-industry

Wang, Yue. (2020). China's $7.6 Trillion Online Payments Market Is No Longer Enough For Jack Ma's Ant Financial. Forbes. Retrieved online: forbes.com/sites/ywang/2020/01/17/ant-financial-is-shifting-away-from-chinas-76-trillion-online-payments-market

Zhu, Julie. (2020). Exclusive: Alibaba's Ant Plans Hong Kong IPO, Targets Valuation Over $200 Billion, Sources Say. Reuters. Retrieved online: reuters.com/article/us-ant-financial-ipo-exclusive/exclusive-alibabas-ant-plans-hong-kong-ipo-targets-valuation-over-200-billion-sources-say-idUSKBN2491JU

3.4 Autonomous Vehicles: Digital Drives

For a complete history of Disneyland's Autopia, visit: davelandweb.com/autopia

A thorough survey of autonomous vehicle safety is available at nhtsa.gov/technology-innovation/automated-vehicles-safety

For an overview of Rapid Flow technology, visit: rapidflowtech.com/surtrac

Audi's take on the congestionless city is available at audi-mediacenter.com/en/press-releases/audi-study-no-congestion-in-the-city-of-the-future-10736

Boudette, Neal E. (2020). Tesla Shines During the Pandemic as Other Automakers Struggle. The New York Times. Retrieved online: nytimes.com/2020/07/02/business/tesla-sales-second-quarter.html

Davies, Chris. (2019). Volvo's Autonomous Trucks Just Picked up Their First Real-World Job. Slashgear. Retrieved online: slashgear.com/volvos-autonomous-trucks-just-picked-up-their-first-real-world-job-14580448

Della Cava, Marco. (2018). Uber Self-Driving Car Kills Arizona Pedestrian, Realizing Worst Fears of the New Tech. USA Today. Retrieved online: usatoday.com/story/tech/2018/03/19/uber-self-driving-car-kills-arizona-woman/438473002

Edelstein, Stephen. (2020). Audi Gives Up on Level 3 Autonomous Driver-Assist System in A8. Motor Authority. Retrieved online: motorauthority.com/news/1127984_audi-gives-up-on-level-3-autonomous-driver-assist-system-in-a8

Gibbs, Samuel. (2018). GM Sued by Motorcyclist in First Lawsuit to Involve Autonomous Vehicle. The Guardian. Retrieved online: theguardian.com/technology/2018/jan/24/general-motors-sued-motorcyclist-first-lawsuit-involve-autonomous-vehicle

Heaps, Russ. (2019). Self-Driving Cars: Honda Remains on Track for Level 3 by 2020. Autotrader. Retrieved online: autotrader.com/car-news/self-driving-cars-honda-remains-track-level-3-2020-281474979945594

McCoy, Kevin. (2017). Drivers Spend an Average of 17 Hours a Year Searching for Parking Spots. USA Today. Retrieved online: usatoday.com/story/money/2017/07/12/parking-pain-causes-financial-and-personal-strain/467637001

Marshall, Aarian. (2020). The Feds Ban a Self-Driving Shuttle Fleet From Carrying People. WIRED. Retrieved online: wired.com/story/feds-ban-self-driving-shuttle-fleet-carrying-people

Shepardson, David. (2017). GM's Self-Driving Cars Involved in Six Accidents in September. Reuters. Retrieved online: reuters.com/article/autos-selfdriving-crashes/gms-self-driving-cars-involved-in-six-accidents-in-september-idUSL2N1MF1RO

Wayland, Michael and Kolodny, Lora. (2020). GM Unveils Cruise Origin Driverless Shuttle. CNBC. Retrieved online: cnbc.com/2020/01/21/gm-subsidiary-cruise-unveils-its-first-purpose-built-autonomous-vehicle.html

Wiggers, Kyle. (2019). Daimler Brings Driverless Truck Tests to Public Roads in Virginia. VentureBeat. Retrieved online: venturebeat.com/2019/09/09/daimler-brings-driverless-truck-tests-to-public-roads-in-virginia

3.5 Government: Phygital for the People

The full landscape of India's Smart City initiative is available at smartcities.gov.in/content

Population data appears courtesy the World Bank Group and World Urbanisation Prospects, United Nations.

Data on U.S. investment in and commitment to digital infrastructure is available at whitehouse.gov/briefings-statements/artificial-intelligence-american-people

Standards for infrastructure delivery management are available at the Global Infrastructure Hub at gihub.org/resources/publications/infrastructure-delivery-management-system-and-standard-for-infrastructure-procurement-and-delivery-management

To review Amazon's stance on its Rekognition program, visit: blog.aboutamazon.com/policy/we-are-implementing-a-one-year-moratorium-on-police-use-of-rekognition

(2018). Government Leans into Machine Learning. GCN. Retrieved online: gcn.com/Articles/2018/08/17/machine-learning.aspx?Page=2

Erickson, David. (2018). Machine Learning, Advanced Search Boosts Cybersecurity. Federal News Network. Retrieved online: federalnewsnetwork.com/federal-insights/2018/09/machine-learning-advanced-search-boosts-cybersecurity

Fazzini, Kate. (2018). Trump's New Strategy Means the U.S. Could Get More Aggressive with Russia and China Over Hacking. CNBC. Retrieved online: cnbc.com/2018/09/21/trump-cybersecurity-policy-offensive-hacking-nsa-russia-china.html

Fonzone, Christopher and Heinzelman, Kate. (2018). Should the Government Regulate Artificial Intelligence? It Already Is. The Hill. Retrieved online: thehill.com/opinion/technology/375606-should-the-government-regulate-artificial-intelligence-it-already-is

Freedman, Andrew. (2017). IBM is Trying to Forecast the Weather on Every Block, Worldwide. *Mashable*. Retrieved online: mashable.com/2017/06/23/ibm-forecast-next-generation-weather-models/#y_rnnCMkwkqq

Goldstein, Phil. (2019). AI Use Poised to Grow in State Government, Survey Finds. *StateTech*. Retrieved online: statetechmagazine.com/article/2019/12/ai-use-poised-grow-state-government-survey-finds

Galston, William A. (2018). Why Government Should Help Shape the Future of AI. Brookings Institution. Retrieved online: brookings.edu/research/why-the-government-must-help-shape-the-future-of-ai

Joshi, Naveen. (2018). 4 Ways Global Defense Forces Use AI. *Forbes*. Retrieved online: forbes.com/sites/cognitiveworld/2018/08/26/4-ways-the-global-defense-forces-are-using-ai/#96ac287503e4

Kanowitz, Stephanie. (2017). Analytics Platform Helps KC Anticipate the Needs of Its Citizens. *GCN*. Retrieved online: gcn.com/articles/2017/06/23/kansas-city-data-integration.aspx

Leonard, Matt. (2018). Deep Learning Quickly Finds Structures Affected by Lava. *GCN*. Retrieved online: gcn.com/articles/2018/07/24/hawaii-volcano-lava-mapping.aspx?m=1

Marr, Bernard. (2018). How Is AI Used in Education – Real World Examples of Today and a Peek into the Future. *Forbes*. Retrieved online: forbes.com/sites/bernardmarr/2018/07/25/how-is-ai-used-in-education-real-world-examples-of-today-and-a-peek-into-the-future/#720648dc586e

Pierobon, Jim. (2018). Next Phase for Chattanooga's Smart Grid: An Airport Microgrid. *Energy News Network*. Retrieved online: energynews.us/2018/03/14/southeast/next-phase-for-chattanoogas-smart-grid-an-airport-microgrid

Van Wagenen, Juliet. (2017). Maryland Taps AI-Backed Traffic Signal Upgrade to Ease Traffic Flows. *StateTech*. Retrieved online: statetechmagazine.com/article/2017/11/maryland-taps-ai-backed-traffic-signal-upgrade-ease-traffic-flows

3.6 Retail: Shopping Everywhere, One Person at a Time

To access numbers on consumer spending in 2020, visit facteus.com/reports/first-report-7-15-2020

For deeper insights from the National Retail Federation on the state of the industry, access cdn.nrf.com/sites/default/files/2020-06/RS-118304%20NRF%20Retail%20Impact%20Report%20.pdf

A quick history of the shift in retail from McKinsey's perspective is available at mckinsey.com/industries/retail/our-insights/how-retailers-can-keep-up-with-consumers

To access a snapshot of brick and mortar's struggles, visit: foxbusiness.com/retail/features-retail-apocalypse-bankruptcy-stores-closing

For Deloitte's take on navigating 2020 from a retail perspective, visit: deloitte.com/content/dam/insights/us/articles/trends-2020/DUP-1025_CP2020_FINAL1.pdf

For more on personalization, access Segment's State of Personalization Report: grow.segment.com/Segment-2017-Personalization-Report.pdf

The PricewaterhouseCoopers results from its annual global consumer insights survey is available at pwc.com/gx/en/industries/consumer-markets/consumer-insights-survey.html

Boudet, Julien, Gregg, Brian, Wong, Jane and Schuler, Gustavo. (2017). What Shoppers Really Want from Personalized Marketing. McKinsey. Retrieved online: mckinsey.com/business-functions/marketing-and-sales/our-insights/what-shoppers-really-want-from-personalized-marketing

Fontanella, Clint. (2020). 15 Examples of Brands with Brilliant Omni-Channel Experiences. Hubspot. Retrieved online: blog.hubspot.com/service/omni-channel-experience

Garcia, Tonya. (2020). Walmart Surpasses eBay in U.S. E-commerce for the First Time, Amazon Still Tops. *MarketWatch*. Retrieved online: marketwatch.com/story/walmart-surpasses-ebay-in-us-e-commerce-for-the-first-time-amazon-still-tops-emarketer-2020-06-15

Grill-Goodman, Jamie. (2017). Target's $550M Retail Technology Investment Ties it Up with Walmart and Amazon in the Delivery Race. *Retail Info Systems*. Retrieved online: risnews.com/targets-550m-retail-technology-investment-ties-it-walmart-and-amazon-delivery-race

O'Shea, Dan. (2018). E-commerce Shoppers Expect Free Shipping, Branded Giveaways. *RetailDive*. Retrieved online: retaildive.com/news/e-commerce-shoppers-expect-free-shipping-branded-giveaways/532349

Samuels, Alana. (2020). Many Companies Won't Survive the Pandemic. Amazon Will Emerge Stronger Than Ever. *TIME* magazine. Retrieved online: time.com/5870826/amazon-coronavirus-jeff-bezos-congress

Sopadjieva, Emma, Dholakia, Utpal M. and Benjamin, Beth. (2017). A Study of 46,000 Shoppers Shows That Omnichannel Retailing Works. *Harvard Business Review*. Retrieved online: hbr.org/2017/01/a-study-of-46000-shoppers-shows-that-omnichannel-retailing-works

Spector, Sean. (2018). Why Same-Day Delivery is a Win-Win for Consumers and Retailers. *TotalRetail*. Retrieved online: mytotalretail.com/article/why-same-day-delivery-is-a-win-win-for-consumers-and-retailers

Tynan, Dan. (2018). Personalization Is a Priority for Retailers, but Can Online Vendors Deliver? *Adweek*. Retrieved online: adweek.com/digital/personalization-is-a-priority-for-retailers-online-and-off-but-its-harder-than-it-looks-in-an-off-the-shelf-world

Walk-Morris, Tatiana. (2020). Retail Sales Spiked Nearly 93% in May. *RetailDive*. Retrieved online: retaildive.com/news/e-commerce-sales-spiked-nearly-93-in-may/579725

3.7 Knowledge Workers: Phygital Wears a White Collar

For a portrait of jobs at the intersection of AI from the Brookings Institution, visit: brookings.edu/wp-content/uploads/2019/11/2019.11.20_BrookingsMetro_What-jobs-are-affected-by-AI_Report_Muro-Whiton-Maxim.pdf

To track advertising spend in the last decade, visit statista.com/statistics/237974/online-advertising-spending-worldwide

For IDC's analysis of AI, visit: idc.com/getdoc.jsp?containerId=prUS45613519

Feiner, Lauren. (2020). Google U.S. Ad Revenue Will Drop for the First Time This Year, eMarketer Says. CNBC. Retrieved online: cnbc.com/2020/06/22/google-ad-revenue-will-drop-this-year-emarketer-says.html

Kostov, Nick and O'Reilly, Lara. (2017). WPP Sounds a Warning Signal on Consumer-Ad Spending; Shares Sink. *The Wall Street Journal*. Retrieved online: wsj.com/articles/wpp-lowers-growth-forecast-as-advertisers-cut-spending-1503474230

Martineau, Kim. (2019). Toward Artificial Intelligence That Learns to Write Code. *MIT News*. Retrieved online: news.mit.edu/2019/toward-artificial-intelligence-that-learns-to-write-code-0614

Price, Penry. (2017). Why Creative Agencies Need to Think Like Consultants in 2017. *AdAge*. Retrieved Online: adage.com/article/digitalnext/creative-agencies-consultants-2017/307400

Reynolds, Matt. (2017). AI Learns to Write Its Own Code by Stealing from Other Programs. *NewScientist*. Retrieved online: newscientist.com/article/mg23331144-500-ai-learns-to-write-its-own-code-by-stealing-from-other-programs

Rittenhouse, Lindsay. (2019). Global Ad Growth to Slow in 2020 Due to Weakening Economy. *AdAge*. Retrieved online: adage.com/article/agency-news/global-ad-growth-slow-2020-due-weakening-economy/2221206

Shields, Mike. (2017). The Future of Ad Agencies Has Never Been More in Doubt. *Business Insider*. Retrieved online: businessinsider.com/companies-are-cutting-out-ad-agencies-and-going-in-house-2017-6

Simonite, Tom. (2017). Google's Learning Software Learns to Write Learning Software. *WIRED*. Retrieved online: wired.com/story/googles-learning-software-learns-to-write-learning-software

Epilogue

Impacts of the tech cold war are adapted and paraphrased from a talk by TPG Co-CEO Jim Coulter for *Bloomberg* that is available at bloomberg.com/news/videos/2019-11-07/tpg-co-ceo-on-global-trends-to-watch-china-tech-esg-video

Conniff, Richard. (2011). What the Luddites Really Fought Against. *Smithsonian Magazine*. Retrieved online: smithsonianmag.com/history/what-the-luddites-really-fought-against-264412

Howell, Elizabeth. (2020). "Deepfake" Nixon Video Discusses A Moon-Landing Disaster That Never Happened. *Forbes*. Retrieved online: forbes.com/sites/elizabethhowell1/2020/07/21/deepfake-nixon-video-discusses-a-moon-landing-disaster-that-never-happened

Nakashima, Ellen. (2019). U.S. Pushes Hard for a Ban on Huawei in Europe, But the Firm's 5G Prices Are Nearly Irresistible. *The Washington Post*. Retrieved online: washingtonpost.com/world/national-security/for-huawei-the-5g-play-is-in-europe--and-the-us-is-pushing-hard-for-a-ban-there/2019/05/28/582a8ff6-78d4-11e9-b7ae-390de4259661_story.html

Russell, Karl. (2020). Big Tech Earnings Surge as Economy Slumps. *The New York Times*. Retrieved online: nytimes.com/live/2020/07/30/business/stock-market-today-coronavirus

About the Author

Vivek Sharma holds extensive experience in building and growing profitable businesses through the application of digital technology. Vivek is the CEO of InStride and previously held leadership roles at The Walt Disney Co., Yahoo! and McKinsey & Co. Vivek is also an adjunct professor of data science at the University of Southern California's Marshall School of Business and is an independent board director for JetBlue Airways. He lives in Southern California with his wife and two children.

CPSIA information can be obtained
at www.ICGtesting.com
Printed in the USA
LVHW011628060121
675887LV00016B/1867